SIMPLY SAUTÉ

SIMPLY sauté

Fast, Easy and Healthy **ITALIAN COOKING**—All in One Pan

SILVIA BIANCO

⊠

MARLOWE & COMPANY
NEW YORK

SIMPLY SAUTÉ: *Fast, Easy and Healthy Italian Cooking—All in One Pan*
Copyright © 2003 by Silvia Bianco
Photographs by Peter Bradley

Published by
Marlowe & Company
An Imprint of Avalon Publishing Group Incorporated
161 William Street, 16th Floor
New York, NY 10038

Library of Congress Cataloging-in-Publication Data

Bianco, Silvia.
Simply sauté : fast, easy and healthy Italian cooking—all in one pan / by Silvia Bianco.
p. cm.
ISBN 1-56924-561-4 (trade paper)
1. Sautéing. 2. Cookery, Italian. 3. Quick and easy cookery. I. Title.
TX689.4 .B53 2002
641.7'7—dc21   2002141435

9 8 7 6 5 4 3 2

Designed by Pauline Neuwirth, Neuwirth & Associates, Inc.

Printed in the United States of America
Distributed by Publishers Group West

*To Biscotti—a special place that became more than just a restaurant
that serves good food and wine.*

*It provided comfort and joy to thousands
who walked through its door.*

*It carried me on a journey that profoundly affected
the person I have become. Thank you.*

Contents

⊠

ix

SIMPLY SAUTÉ

⌧

Author's Note

AS *SIMPLY SAUTÉ* arrives in bookstores in December of 2003, my restaurant, Biscotti, which inspired most of the recipes in this book, will have approached the end of its 10-year lease. Coincidence? I don't think so. Synchronistic? Absolutely. What is the meaning of this? Beats me! Could this mean that there may be another Biscotti opening sometime, somewhere? Possibly. What I do know for sure is that this is symbolic of "one door closing as another opens," and Biscotti will always live on in the pages of this book.

INTRODUCTION
Sauté—An Ideal Way to Cook Almost Anything

⊠

OUR LOVE AFFAIR with Italian food is in full swing. If you're looking for a book on traditional Italian cooking, there are many wonderful ones to choose from. This is not one of them. *Simply Sauté* is, rather, my personal way of cooking Italian food, which I have had the privilege of cooking thousands of times for thousands of my restaurant patrons over the last ten years. It is an expression of my love affair with my native food.

What *most* distinguishes this cookbook from the many others available to choose and cook from is this: Every recipe, from entrées and side dishes to appetizers and desserts, is sautéed.

Sauté, a technique in which the cook browns or cooks ingredients in a small amount of hot oil in a sauté or frying pan, usually for only a few minutes, is prevalent in Italian, as well as French cooking. Yet, somewhat mystifyingly, sauté is not a commonly practiced cooking technique in every American home, the way, say, roasting or grilling is. Rather, sauté continues to be practiced most widely by professional chefs. I'm willing to bet you that in virtually every restaurant in America, on every night of the week, no matter what cuisine is being served, at least one chef in the kitchen is standing in front of a stove flipping a sauté pan over a flame.

I always ask students in my cooking classes if they sauté food at home. Invariably, 25 to 30 percent of the hands go up. When I probe further and ask *what* they sauté, almost all answer "vegetables." Some say they sauté chicken cutlets. Most don't exactly know what sauté is. They think it's frying. Their explanations and reactions seem to indicate that they don't even consider sautéing anything other than a side dish. The concept of putting various ingredients together in one pan and having them all cooked perfectly at the same time is just not how they plan a meal. They believe it would be too difficult. (One theory I have about this reluctance: It's all those cooking shows featuring chefs flipping all those sauté pans. My goodness, you have to be an acrobat with split-second timing!) It is far easier, for example, to put a large cut of meat or a pan of filleted fish in the oven and shut the door, or to place large pieces of food on the grill: Turn them over once and they're soon ready.

My students are always stunned to see how easy it is to sauté. Sauté is significantly economical, fast, healthy, and fun. It is, frankly, an ideal way to cook almost anything. It offers the cook an open invitation to create an endless variety of delicious meals in a single pan on a stovetop and, in the process, to bring out the most flavor from almost any type of food. The results are dishes that please and stimulate our senses, nourish our bodies, and comfort our spirit.

Italian food is the ultimate comfort food. If you were to ask a thousand Americans of all ages, from all parts of the country, what their favorite type of food is, I would confidently guess that the overwhelming majority would say Italian. Yet only within the last thirty years have we begun to know and appreciate it as an authentic cuisine. The appearance of Ada Boni's *Italian Regional Cooking,* published in Italy in 1969 and soon thereafter in the United States, was a watershed event that influenced not only professional chefs in America, but also Italian women cooking at home for their families. It was published at a time when Italians, on a mass scale, were discovering for the first time the diversity and richness of their cuisine. As late as the 1950s, most Italians ate and were familiar with their local fare only. To understand why this is so, it is important to recognize that Italy did not become a unified country until 1861. In that year only 600,000 of Italy's then 25 million people spoke the national language. The majority of Italians spoke only their particular dialect—versions of Italian that were not easily understood by fellow Italians from other regions.

The unification of Italy brought together twenty distinctive regions in the north and south, including the islands of Sicily and Sardinia, all with their own local customs and distinctive cuisines. "Travelers would have been able to recognize which

region they were in simply from the type of food they found," writes Giorgio Mistretta, in his wonderful book *The Italian Gourmet*. Since Italy was a predominantly agricultural country until after World War II, local crops and specific traditions of food preparation determined the cuisine. Italians tended to be (and still are) very specific about what ingredients, herbs, and spices went into their local specialties and deviations were seldom tolerated.

Recipes or, more often, hands–on demonstrations of how to cook family meals and special provincial dishes were passed on, most often, from mother to daughter, generation after generation, for cooking was mostly the responsibility of women. Women were the masters of the family kitchen. It was not uncommon for grandmothers, mothers, and daughters to spend a large portion of each day in the kitchen preparing meals and stocking pantries with food picked from their gardens or brought home by their husbands, sons, and fathers, who worked on farms. Today, these women are grandmothers in their 70s, 80s, and 90s, and their recipes and traditions are quickly becoming a dying art as their daughters, like women everywhere, leave the kitchen to work outside the home. Still, food continues to hold great importance in the lives of most Italians, so the old recipes and techniques continue to be passed on, only now they are made using modern appliances. This, of course, changes the taste somewhat, but not the intentions behind the preparations. They are still prepared with a love of food and a desire to please and satisfy the diner.

Distinctive regional differences still prevail throughout Italy, but over the last fifty years advances in transportation, communication, and education have exposed the richness and variety of Italian cuisine, not only to other Italians, but also to the world.

I became a professional chef in 1993 when my husband and I opened our restaurant, Biscotti, in Ridgefield, Connecticut. Corwyn had worked in at least forty-five restaurants on both the East and West coasts in almost every capacity. As for me, most of my professional "restaurant" experience came from working in snack bars and local family restaurants as a waitress throughout high school, college, and part of graduate school. The first restaurant I worked in was Chef Antonio's, in Mamaroneck, New York. I grew up in Harrison, New York, the next town over, which had a large Italian population, so Chef Antonio's was usually packed. It did a good job serving up traditional Italian-American fare: eggplant parmigiana, chicken marsala, linguine in white or red clam sauce, although I don't remember much about how that kitchen worked. I was fourteen and dazzled by the fast pace of a restaurant and hooked on how much money I could make working as a bus girl. When I was fifteen, I got a summer job working at the snack bar at Rye Beach Playland. I scooped ice cream or got bags of chips for crowds of kids, three deep around the counter. One of the most memorable requests that summer was from a twelve year old who asked for "a waitress to go, with nothing on it."

The next summer I worked at another snack bar, this time at the private pool and beach club of the Westchester Country Club. I worked for Mrs. McDenney, a hard-driving Irish women who, because of my experience working at a fast paced counter, had me working the cold sandwich line while she cooked the hamburgers, hot dogs, and grilled reubens. This is where I first learned "the dance"—something practiced by every good server or line cook—and the notion that every step serves a purpose.

This experience came in handy the summer after my freshman year in college. I was eighteen and wanted to live in Montauk, at the eastern tip of Long Island. I got a job at the then-private Montauk Golf and Racket Club. At night I was a waitress in their dining room. By day I worked at the snack bar by the pool as a short-order cook. One day the general manager of the resort was expecting eight to ten businessmen for a private lunch meeting, and the restaurant chef didn't show up. He pulled me out of the snack bar and into the large restaurant kitchen and told me to make something. I made a tomato and onion salad, an assortment of cold sandwiches, and a quick tomato and basil soup with little pasta shells. It must have been good because for the rest of the summer I was the general manager's hero. I had no professional cooking experience, except for this one-day stint, and no formal culinary training.

My training came from experiences in my mother's kitchen, interspersed with visits to my grandmother's kitchen in Calabria, the region in southwestern Italy that occupies the "toe" of Italy's "boot." I was born in Italy but moved to America along with my mother and siblings when I was five, to join my father. I was almost immediately thrust into American culture when I started school shortly after arriving in the United States, but at home, my life and my mother's kitchen were distinctly Italian. My native Italian dialect was the only language spoken at home, and around the kitchen table the meals we ate remained remarkably similar to the ones we shared in Italy—pasta e fagioli, escarole in chicken broth with little meatballs, pasta with tomato sauce and fresh basil, broccoli rabe and sausage.

On Sundays, the kitchen became my father's domain. My brothers and I woke up to the aroma of pork spareribs and meatballs browning in a large pot in preparation for the puréed tomatoes that would soon be added to it. To this day, that aroma still evokes the memory of my father standing in front of the stove thoroughly enjoying his time in the kitchen. His wonderful meat sauce, which would top a huge platter of pasta, was simply called the gravy, and my father made it with such perfection, from personally selecting the meat from the local butcher, making the meatballs, selecting the tomatoes and the pasta, and serving it (with my help, of course) to our family of eight. This was accompanied by another platter of fresh vegetables and a salad of mixed greens, or, in the summer, a tomato and onion salad, made from tomatoes grown in our garden, chopped and drizzled with extra virgin olive oil and sprinkled with fresh basil. As in Italy, the meal usually ended with fresh fruit and nuts.

My mother cooked the meals the rest of the week. She also baked bread twice a week, only now she used an indoor gas oven instead of the outdoor wood-burning one she shared with my grandmother in Italy. The tomato sauce we ate came from mason jars we kept in a pantry in the cellar. Every September my mother and I spent days, along with my aunts' help, canning bushels of tomatoes bought from local farmers. The pantry also held jars of pickled eggplant, marinated mushrooms, and roasted peppers. Handmade sausages and sopresata hung drying from wooden poles that were fastened beneath the ceiling. Sardines packed in salt and dried figs stuffed with walnuts also lined the shelves. Hot red chili peppers were strung together to form a long, colorful rope. And, whereas in Italy they were hung to dry on a warm, sunny balcony, in our new home they were hung to dry near the warm boiler in the cellar. Our basement—or cellar, as we called it—had a second kitchen and a huge table we used to make our numerous food preparations. We had a virtual food factory going on in that cellar. I remember thinking how delicious all of the delicacies we made were, and I felt luckier than other kids who had to eat American food, whatever that was. I thought that, some day, this food ought to be discovered by Americans. I was amused when years later I saw what I had thought of as my family's peasant food displayed and selling as gourmet at fancy food stores like Balducci's in Manhattan.

Wine, which is a required accompaniment to any Italian meal, was also homemade by my father and kept in large wood barrels and recycled glass bottles in a cement cellar he built under the back porch. The back yard was also devoted to a large vegetable garden, an oasis of tomatoes, eggplant, zucchini, basil, and parsley, and even a couple of fig trees that my father buried in the ground every October, before the first frost, and resurrected every spring. As in Italy, our pantry, cellars, and garden provided the ingredients for tasty meals all year long.

Food, just as it was in Italy, was still the focus of my family's social life, and it called for frequent gatherings in the kitchen to prepare it and in the dining room to share it. My mother's kitchen was constantly filled with my aunts or her friends getting together to make bread, or cookies, or fresh pasta. Pasta, my favorite, was usually made with dough rolled thin using a three-foot rolling pin my father made from a wooden rod specifically designed for this purpose. The dough was perfect when it resembled an extra large, thin pizza. The dough was rolled around the rolling pin that was then pulled out leaving compact layers of dough that could then easily be cut with a knife to form fettuccine. Sometimes we made *a maccaroni al ferro*, a long pasta with a small hole running through it, similar to bucatini, that was made by rolling each strand of pasta dough around a thin metal rod. No pasta that comes from a machine ever tasted like this. Sometimes my relatives would gather to make polenta, which was served on a large, wooden cutting board set at the center of the table and topped with sautéed ground pork in a tomato sauce. Each diner gathered around the table and ate from the communal 'plate' and began his or her turn—usually determined by who spoke the loudest—telling tales of the old days in Italy.

A continuous influx of cooks gathered in my mother's kitchen, and I watched what they did and I listened to the stories they told. I was mesmerized. When they cooked, they rarely followed a recipe. Instead they casually kept an eye on the food as they socialized and determined instinctually when it needed to be stirred or turned, adding a little of this and a little of that as they went along. When I was put to work peeling potatoes, peeling shrimp, or kneading dough, I did so gladly, enjoying the intoxicating aromas, reveling in the easy comfort, and joining in the laughter that took place in the kitchen. Year after year, the kitchen was where I felt most at home, so I naturally sought out and was taught the secrets of this special group of masters.

When I moved into my first apartment in Manhattan, I had just come from having spent a year living in Ravenna, a provincial city in the region of Emilia Romagna on Italy's northern Adriatic coast, safe haven to Dante and some of the greatest Byzantine art ever created. I had just graduated from college and wanted to spend some time in my native country, so I studied art at the Accademia di Belle Arte. I lived with a prominent Italian family who employed a young, talented chef, so I dined at delicious, multicourse meals where I was exposed to Italian food I had never known. Finally, with a kitchen of my own, I took to producing lavish buffets and dinner parties, often recreating some of the dishes that I had enjoyed in Ravenna. I made lasagna with béchamel instead of using ricotta the way my mother taught me. (Today, in my restaurant, I make lasagna with both béchamel and ricotta. I use béchamel for the creaminess it adds, and ricotta for its texture and taste.) I also made tortellini in brodo (chicken broth) and perfected my bolognese sauce to the ranks of the divine. The meals I made didn't strike me as onerous to produce because I loved preparing them and sharing the results with my friends and family. It was what I did for fun.

For a profession, I worked in the fashion industry while I went to school at night for an MBA in marketing. When I graduated, I got a sales executive job in the telecommunications industry. My job gave me valuable experience and the flexible hours I needed to raise my two young children, Teresa and Mathew. But it wasn't wholly satisfying. Then their father, my first husband, Robert, died suddenly in 1989. I was left to raise my children alone, so I spent a couple more years in the same job, but my dissatisfaction grew. I knew there was a purpose to my life, but the job I had wasn't bringing me any closer to finding it. One night, in total surrender, I literally dropped to my knees and declared my willingness to fulfill that purpose in whatever capacity life had in store for me. I didn't care how. All I asked was to be given the opportunity to share the gifts I had to offer, whatever they were.

A couple of years later I was remarried and opening my restaurant, Biscotti, in Ridgefield, Connecticut, with my new husband, Corwyn. Although it might appear as if my life suddenly took a dramatic turn—and in many ways it did—starting a restaurant was actually a natural move for the both of us. We were both dissatisfied with our jobs and fantasized often about opening a restaurant in the country. Corwyn had plenty of experience in the restaurant business and had sampled my cooking countless times so, unlike myself, he never had any doubts that I could do the cooking.

I could not fully understand then that starting a restaurant was, in part, an answer to my prayers. It would lead me on a journey of discovery, both culinary and personal, that would dramatically reshape my life. But, more simply than that, opening Biscotti was the backdrop for my love affair with sauté. This is where the story of my restaurant and my cooking style begins.

Two weeks before we were to open Biscotti, I visited the Maryland restaurant of some *paisans*—salt-of-the-earth "country people"—fellow Italians and good friends. There was nothing rustic about their beautiful restaurant kitchen, with its twelve-burner stove, three pizza ovens, long stainless steel prep tables, and stacks of sauté pans. Directly across from the burners was a long refrigerator unit filled with drawers holding vegetables, condiments, poultry, fish, and other frequently used ingredients. In that kitchen I stood engrossed, watching as the cooks prepared the evening's meals. Their every movement served a purpose: The sauté cook would pull open a drawer, grab a handful of ingredients, and add them to one or more hot sauté pans. He'd then grab another pan or two and turn the sizzling ingredients in the pan with a couple of easy, flowing tosses. He'd add stock to one pan, pasta to another one—maybe some wine to still another—sending flames soaring from the pan. Soon some of the pans would come off the burners, to be handed to another cook who would carefully pull the ingredients from the pan onto a waiting warmed plate.

They moved with the grace of dancers, and although I didn't yet know how to do just what they were doing, I felt, in every bone in my body, the rhythm of the dance and the possibilities of what could go into the pan. With ideas for sautéed dishes dancing in my head, I began that very night to rework the menu we had planned to present to Biscotti's first patrons. Sauté became the technical foundation on which we would build our restaurant.

My restaurant kitchen wasn't, to put it mildly, as well equipped as that of my restaurant friends in Maryland. At seventy-two square feet—all of twelve feet by six feet—it was smaller than many bathrooms in New York City apartments. The stove had four gas burners. Next to it was a deep fryer, which we converted to a pasta cooker. It also had a small under-counter refrigerator, a freezer, and, around the corner, a small walk-in refrigerator—although, to be more accurate, you could really only lean into it.

Describe this set-up to someone in the restaurant business, and they'll tell you I was crazy, that there was no way you could feed an evening's worth of meals to the patrons of a fifty-seat dining room from this kitchen. I suspect they secretly thought that it would take a miracle for us to even make it through that first winter (we opened in November 1993, during the coldest winter in Connecticut history). It had never occurred to me—an inexperienced sauté cook using a four-burner stove to serve up an almost completely sauté menu, made-to-order for 50 to 100 or more patrons a night—that what I had set out to do couldn't be done.

For months, my stomach ached from nerves as I stood in front of that stove, waiting for the first orders of the night to come in. To prepare myself, I insisted on being meticulously organized about the prep work: I placed most of the ingredients I would need in uniform containers set in iced bins, lined up within arm's reach on the counter behind me.

As the restaurant started to fill up, the orders came in with a speed that could easily send me into a panic—and sometimes it did—but I did everything I could to remain focused on the task at hand. Only the task! Corwyn would say that there could have been a fire around me and I wouldn't have noticed.

To calm my nerves I nightly gave myself a silent pep talk. I reminded myself that whenever I was under pressure to cook for others, whether I was preparing a family meal or a buffet for 50 guests, I did so almost effortlessly, and the results were always enjoyed and appreciated. I kept those successes in mind. Making good food was part of who I was. Now, all I had to do was trust that I could do it again. I willed it to work. We had everything invested in the restaurant. Failure, as they say, was simply not an option.

Ten years later, now with eight burners and two sauté cooks on the cooking line, Biscotti has thrived, and I marvel at what we've accomplished. It is, if nothing else, a testament to what you can make happen if you're determined and focused on a goal—in spite of the obstacles—by holding onto a dream, a vision etched clearly in your mind and felt authentically in your spirit. You can do anything. This is the place where miracles are created.

The recipes in *Simply Sauté* do not represent the usual Italian fare etched into the American consciousness, nor do they follow a simple binary distinction between northern and southern Italian cuisine. Though I realize we have come a long way from the "spaghetti and meatballs" understanding of Italian cuisine, and are now familiar with dishes from many regions of Italy, especially Tuscany, I am still asked constantly, "Is the food served at your restaurant northern or southern Italian?" The answer is, of course, neither. Though I am certainly influenced by all the traditional regional, country cuisines of Italy, the particular sensibility of each recipe varies, and with each one I've sought inspiration from a variety of sources.

I draw constantly on Old World influences—the flavors, ingredients, and taste combinations that have evolved over decades, even centuries, in traditional Italian kitchens—both in homes and restaurants. Although my cooking is particularly influenced by the rustic, flavorful cooking of my native Calabria, as was taught to me by my mother, grandmother, father, and the assortment of aunts and family friends, I also draw on a variety of other regional Italian tastes. Over the past ten years, I have discovered and now enjoy cooking with the exquisite pesto sauces that originated in the Liguria, with Gorgonzola from Piedmont, mascarpone from Lombardy, and polenta from the Veneto, the region around Venice. I have become enamored of the fresh pasta from Emilia Romagna, the intense flavors and simple tomato sauces of Campania and Calabria, and the fruits of Sicily. Importers around the United States are helping to bring specialty Italian ingredients onto more grocery shelves than ever before; what was once available, if at all, only on the shelves of small neighborhood Italian grocers, is now available on supermarket shelves nationwide—so finding excellent specialty ingredients to cook with is easier than ever.

Essentially, I cook by instinct. I am still unsure of exactly where many of my ideas for new dishes come from. It's as though a form of alchemy or magic takes place that inspires me to use one ingredient with another in a particular way. I rarely know ahead of time what I'll do for that evening's specials beyond the cut of meat, type of fish, or seasonal produce I ordered. I simply look to use the freshest ingredients in simple, uncomplicated ways.

Like many women in Italy who carry on the tradition of shopping each day for the main ingredients they'll cook with later that day, my ingredients—though they are ordered the day before from vendors chosen for their specific specialties—are the ingredients I will use for that day's menu items and specials. I get to inspect, smell, and touch the produce, the cheese, the meat, and the fish that come into the restaurant. I experiment constantly with new ingredients, adding them in varying combinations to my sauté pan to create a new sauce for pasta or a risotto to stuff the trout that just came in, or a filling for the hand-rolled lasagna we make every day.

My habit of passing around samples of my latest innovation is well known amongst my staff and regular customers. This is the part of cooking I like best, inventing a new dish or a new twist on an old dish and seeing others enjoy it. Ultimately, this is the only true way to judge if the food you cook is wonderful, not whether you properly carry out the instructions of a particular recipe or cooking method.

I believe I owe a large part of the success of my particular style of cooking to the fact that I never learned the rules of professional cooking. And having never learned them, I break them constantly. I am convinced that there are many dishes I would never have attempted if I knew the rules. I learned by trial and error at the restaurant.

I simply observed how food looked and tasted after I treated it a certain way, and made the necessary adjustments. Still, it helps to learn basic cooking techniques, for they guide you toward an understanding of the best ways to treat different foods, and in the process free you to experiment with your own favorite ingredients in creative ways. Sauté is ideal because it is an easy technique to learn.

Fundamentally, I am less preoccupied with preserving the specific culinary traditions that characterize the way food is prepared within a particular region of Italy. Many other food advocates and cookbook writers have, justifiably, taken this as their cause. Instead, I am committed to the idea of drawing widely on those same traditions, to create dishes that please the palates of today's diners.

I particularly depart from traditional Italian cooking when it comes to many of the sauces I use, and how I use them. Essentially, I like to create a sauce that responds to the wonderful flavors emerging from the sauté pan. I do this by combining sauces or adding different broths and stocks to the ingredients sautéing in the pan. (I started to do this when I realized that the liquid in the pan was simply not enough to coat the pasta.) You would be hard pressed, for instance, to find pasta with tomato-pesto sauce on any restaurant menu in Italy. At Biscotti, tomato-pesto is an essential sauce—one that appears in at least one dish on every menu I've ever offered. I have even taken the basics of this simple sauce further by combining tomato, pesto, sherry, and a hint of cream, and incorporating them into a delicious sauce for sautéed chicken, scallops, or shrimp.

Over the years, as I became more familiar with the sauces of classic French cooking, I discovered that the basic cooking strategy I evolved at Biscotti owed its debts to longstanding French cooking traditions. In that regard, I take some satisfaction in following, albeit not singlemindedly, in the footsteps of the cooks of the court of Catherine de Medici. Catherine is widely credited with establishing the basics of French cooking when, journeying from Florence to France to marry Henry II in 1533, she brought her Tuscan cooks with her. The cooks of the French court, it's believed, adapted the techniques of their new Italian colleagues and went on to add their own creative touches, soon overtaking their teachers' skills and giving birth to what we now regard as classic French cuisine.

There is a lesson here about the power of synthesizing culinary traditions. I like to think that I have come full circle and, that by making my own contemporary version of Italian cuisine, I also honor French traditions. For years I've secretly feared that traditionalists would discover my heresy and deem my food not Italian, or at least not Italian *enough*! Now, in an odd way, I feel redeemed, for it is truly Italian in origin. Today, I completely accept that how I cook can honor Italian cuisine, which I love passionately, and yet I can still push the envelope of tradition, and create tastes that please our modern palates with a cooking technique that doesn't require hours in front of the stove.

⊠

Most of the recipes in this book have been created for the customers of Biscotti, and they have been served thousands of times. I've also taught many of them to hundreds of students who have attended my cooking classes. Recipes, of course, aren't static: We continue to refine dishes all the time at our restaurant. But the recipes I include in this book have withstood the test of time. They have delighted countless diners, and I'm confident they will delight you and those for and with whom you cook. They also present a wide array of taste sensations and flavor combinations. A restaurant must cater to customers' varying tastes every night. One customer may want, for example, the chicken and asparagus dish (page 56) to be made with string beans instead of asparagus, while another may want you to leave out the bacon or to use pork instead of chicken. Whatever the particular demands of my restaurant patrons or your family, the sauté pan can be a virtual palette of varying ingredients, added in or left out.

All of the recipes in this book had to meet another key criterion: They must, by necessity, be prepared easily and speedily. Anyone who has had to wait too long for a meal to come out of a restaurant's kitchen recognizes that chefs don't have all night to prepare a dish. We are usually under strict time limits to put out a meal so that the table being served can complete their meal in time for the next seating. To that end, each recipe has a cooking time of ten minutes or less and a preparation time of thirty minutes or less.

⊠

But no matter how I interpret what I do, I acknowledge that the way I cook has led me to create recipes that tend to break from one or another tradition, and that come with no easy label. This way of cooking is, I have come to realize, simply sauté.

I hope you'll be as fascinated with sauté as I have been for the past ten years, and that you, too, will be inspired by a whole new world of possibilities you can create in a single pan in your kitchen.

SAUTÉ **basics**
What to Know, What to Have

⊠

Thirteen Things You Should Know before You Get Started

SAUTÉ IS A simple, quick, and highly flavorful way of preparing a meal. To sauté means to add any ingredient to a small amount of hot oil to brown or cook it, along with some flavorings, in a sauté or frying pan. Sauté can be done with small, uniform pieces of any meat, fish, or vegetable. It's not very mysterious. In fact, many of you probably use this technique from time to time without even realizing it. Even so, sauté is not widely recognized as a method that can be used to create an entire meal for two, four, or more people. But, just by following a few guidelines, you can use sauté for a surprising variety of purposes. This book is dedicated to showing you how.

1. You don't need much. The only equipment you need is a sauté pan—also called a skillet or a frying pan—and something to stir with. Sauté pans come in all sizes. I recommend that you use a 7-inch pan for single-serving dishes, a 10-inch pan for double servings, and a 13-inch pan for larger meals.

2. What kind of sauté pan? The best kind is stainless steel, which distributes the heat evenly and cleans well. A coated nonstick sauté pan does not work nearly as well because its surface will not brown and sear the food. (Those pans are great, though, for omelets and frittatas, foods that you *want* to slide off the pan easily, without browning, and for low fat cooking.) Another reason you don't want to use a nonstick pan is that bits of food will not stick to the pan during the cooking process. Those bits, once incorporated into the sauce, will add flavor to the sauces that you will create from the sautéed ingredients. A sauté pan can be straight-edged or sloped. I prefer the sloped pans for two reasons. First, tossing the ingredients is easier in a sloped pan. Second, a sloped pan makes it easier to incorporate into the sauce all the juices and bits of food that may otherwise get stuck in the edges of the straight-edge skillet.

3. Don't overstir. A common mistake made by inexperienced sauté cooks is overstirring, which prevents meat, fish, or other ingredients from searing and browning, and that gets in the way of your locking in the natural flavors. Simply place your ingredients into the hot oil and leave them alone until the undersides of the meat or fish pieces begin to turn opaque (white) and your vegetables brown. Then turn them. All this usually takes no more than 2 minutes.

4. Give some vegetables a head start. Parboil dense vegetables (broccoli, asparagus, etc.) in boiling water for a few minutes to soften them before sautéing, then quickly dunk them in cold water to prevent overcooking. This will ensure that the insides of the vegetables are cooked without the outsides becoming overly brown or burnt.

5. It's not frying. Sautéing and frying are vastly different, so don't use—or think— of the words interchangeably. Sautéing uses a little bit of oil, which becomes part of your sauce. Frying uses lots of oil, which you want kept out of your food. Always start sautéing with a small amount of olive oil, just enough to cover the bottom of the sauté pan. This usually means 3 or 4 tablespoons, perhaps a bit more or less, depending on the size of the pan. Allow the oil to heat, usually for about 30 seconds, before you add the ingredients. The sizzle that you hear when you add an ingredient indicates that the oil is ready. If the oil starts to smoke, it means that the oil is too hot, so remove the pan from the heat for a few moments until the oil cools. Return the oil to the heat and add a small amount of the first ingredient. If the oil begins to sizzle, it's ready. If not, let it heat for a few more seconds. I do not recommend using butter at this point, for butter burns easily over high heat and will turn brown before most of the ingredients in the pan are cooked. However, if you are making a quick sauce with ingredients such as spinach, which cooks in seconds, and you want to use butter instead of olive oil, go right ahead. Here's a tip that all you butter aficionados will love: Adding a small amount of butter, usually a teaspoon or less, is sufficient, at the very end of your sautéed dish. A small amount, at this time will go a long way toward adding butter flavor, without the high cholesterol.

6. Be gentle with garlic. If your recipe calls for minced garlic, add it just before you add a cold or room-temperature ingredient, such as tomatoes, wine, or broth. Finely chopped garlic can burn in less than a minute in hot oil and ruin your entire dish before you even get started. Following with cold ingredients will cool everything down in the pan and prevent burning.

7. Prep everything first. Because sauté is such a quick cooking method, have all your ingredients—broths, sauces etc.—chopped, dredged, defrosted, and ready to go. If something is not ready, remove the pan from the heat while you complete the additional prep.

8. Be uniform. Always cut the ingredients you plan to use into pieces of equal size. That way, they'll cook evenly. For example, chicken must be cut or pounded into relatively thin pieces, but their thickness must be the same. This will allow the chicken to cook thoroughly in a few minutes without overcooking some pieces and undercooking others (a potential mistake with ingredients like chicken or pork).

9. Pasta needs its space. Always cook a pound of pasta in at least 4 quarts of water. It needs room to grow. I like to add a teaspoon of salt, to hasten the boiling time of the water and salt the pasta, and a tablespoon of olive oil when cooking a thin or delicate pasta, such as linguine or angel hair, to prevent the pasta from sticking and clumping together.

10. Dredging can help. Dredging an ingredient—chicken, vegetables, crabcakes, whatever—means coating it in something, usually flour (bleached or unbleached, white or whole wheat) or another dry ingredient, such as breadcrumbs or cornmeal, before sautéing. Dredging gives an ingredient a wonderful, even coating that browns beautifully.

11. More than a pretty face. Many of the recipes in this book call for fresh, chopped Italian (flat-leaf) parsley. One reason is aesthetic. Parsley adds color and makes almost any dish look great. The other is flavor. Unlike basil, which also adds color but has a much stronger taste, parsley adds a subtle flavor that will complement most dishes.

12. Deglazing adds wonderful flavor. A great way to add flavor to your sauces is to deglaze your skillet. Deglazing is simple. It means adding a liquid (usually a wine or liquor) to a pan to lift the browned pieces of meat, fish, etc., that have stuck to the pan. Deglazing adds wonderful flavor to your dish. Normally you remove the large ingredients from the pan before adding the desired liquid to make a sauce. In most of my recipes, I find it unnecessary to remove the ingredients from the pan to make a sauce. It is easier, and more flavorful, to leave them in the pan, make your sauce, and let all your ingredients begin to absorb some of the juices and sauce before you serve the dish.

13. Have fun. The most important rule of all is to remember that cooking is an art, not a science. So have fun with it. You may like tomatoes, while I like potatoes. You like artichokes. I like asparagus. You like white sauces. I like red. You get the picture. Use what you like and create your own masterpieces.

Thirteen Pantry Essentials

1. Olive Oil. Olive oil is sold in several grades. I recommend using extra virgin olive oil, the best grade, for sautéing, and a blended olive oil (such as olive oil blended with canola oil) for frying. In sauté, you want to incorporate the olive oil into your sauce, so that's the place to use the best. When frying, you're using a large quantity of hot oil and you want the food to absorb as little oil as possible, so a blended oil is fine. Olives are harvested, cleaned in water, crunched, and then cold-pressed to squeeze out their oil. Extra virgin olive oil is derived from the very first cold-pressing of the olives without being refined in any way. So this oil not only has an acidity level of less than 1 percent, but it also maintains all the minerals, vitamins, and sediments that are in the olives. This gives the oil a stronger olive taste and a greener color than you'll find in the lower grades, where the oil has gone through multiple cold-pressings and has been refined, producing a product that loses the natural flavor and nutrients in the olives.

2. Canned Tomatoes. Supermarkets carry a variety of canned tomatoes so vast that it can make your head spin. So what should you keep on hand? My rule of thumb (with a few exceptions that I will give you later) is that the less that's done to the tomatoes, the better. That rule eliminates all canned sauces, purées, and pastes. If you stick to peeled, crushed, or diced tomatoes, you are starting with tomatoes (and very little else) that have not been overprocessed. So your sauce will not have a processed taste. Experiment with products from various manufacturers, find one or two that you like (and there are many good ones), and stick with them. An exception to my rule of not using products that have been more than minimally processed is a canned tomato product that's labeled "kitchen ready" or "recipe ready." These products have been cooked before they are canned and result in a delicious sauce in a fraction of the time (usually no more than half an hour). They are readily available from a variety of manufacturers in most supermarkets. I always have my home pantry stocked with these products, as well as with other canned tomatoes. They let me make a sauce in a pinch.

3. Pasta. Here, especially, the varieties are mind-boggling. And they have such foreign names! Though there are literally hundreds of different pastas in all shapes, sizes, and varieties, below is a partial list of the most common varieties:

- Angel hair (or *capelli di angelo*). Thin strands of spaghetti-like pasta.
- Bucatini. Long strands, thicker than spaghetti, with a small hole though the center.
- Cannelloni. Large, thick, round pasta tubes, usually stuffed.
- Conchiglie. Tiny pasta shells, usually used in a broth.
- Ditali. Short tubes, usually used for *pasta e fagioli* (pasta and beans). It also makes an interesting pasta salad.
- Farfalle. Pasta in the shape of bows. Kids love them.
- Fettuccine. Long, flat pasta strands.
- Fusilli. Long or short twists of pasta with a variety of uses.
- Gemelli (literally means "twins"). Two short strands of pasta, twisted together to look like twins.
- Lasagna. Long, wide, flat strands of pasta used to make the familiar baked dish of the same name.

- Linguine. Long, flat strands of pasta, not as wide as fettuccine, but usually of the same thickness. In the category of long pasta, this is my personal favorite, for it holds the sauce better than spaghetti but is not as heavy as fettuccine. And it can be used for almost any variety of sauce.
- Orecchiette. Ear-shaped pasta disks. Great for pasta salads
- Penne. Quill-shaped small pasta tubes
- Penne rigate. Same as "penne" but with ridges, making it better at holding sauces. This, like linguine, fettuccine, and rigatoni, is a staple in my restaurant and in my home.
- Rigatoni. Thick, ridged tubes.
- Spaghetti. Fine to medium strands of rounded pasta.
- Tagliarini. Thin, ribbon-like strands, similar to fettuccine.
- Tagliatelle. Broad ribbon-like strands, usually wider than fettuccine.

Now we must consider another pasta question: Do we use fresh or dry pasta? This really is a matter of personal preference, for both are delicious. At the restaurant, after going back and forth over this question, and after a great deal of experimenting, I found that I could not cook short pastas al dente (cooked, but still firm) if they were fresh. Because overcooked pasta will destroy a dish, I decided to use dry pasta for the short pastas, such as penne and rigatoni (sometimes called macaroni) and fresh pasta for all of my long pastas, such as linguine, spaghetti, and fettuccine. Fresh pasta cooks in 2 to 3 minutes, while dry pasta can take anywhere from 8 to 15 minutes, depending on its thickness.

That brings me to the next important point about pasta. The right pasta must be paired with the right sauce. Thin, delicate pasta, such as angel hair, needs a thin, light sauce, such as oil and garlic or a light fresh tomato sauce. An alfredo sauce or a bolognese sauce, for example, would overwhelm this pasta. On the other hand, those sauces are perfect for thicker, heavier pastas such as fettuccine, rigatoni, and penne.

4. Anchovies. Everyone loves to hate those hairy little fish, yet no Italian pantry is complete without them. Even if you dislike anchovies, I highly recommend that you use them when they are called for in a recipe, especially in marinara sauce. Anchovies add essential flavor to a sauce or dish without necessarily adding a fishy taste. If you really hate the look of them, use anchovy paste, for this is what the anchovies become after they are cooked. Most anchovies in this country come packed in oil, in an oval-shaped tin or glass jar. They can remain on your pantry shelf forever—until they are opened. Then they must be refrigerated.

5. **Chicken Broth.** It's a good idea to keep a few cans of chicken broth (low sodium if you prefer) or chicken bouillon (which needs to be mixed with water) on hand. You will almost always need it to add a bit of liquid or flavor to something you are sautéing, and it's perfect for doing so. The same applies to vegetable broth (see page 230), vegetable bouillon, and fish broth (see page 229). Keep in mind, however, that when using chicken broth in your sauces, the longer they reduce, the more concentrated their flavor and, therefore, the more noticeable the saltiness. You can compensate for this in a number of ways by using low sodium brands, by making your own broth (see page 228), by diluting commercial broth with additional water, or by simply adding a bit of water to your reduced sauce.

6. **Arborio Rice.** A short-grain rice used to make risotto because of its creaminess and ability to absorb all cooking liquid while still retaining its firm texture. All risotto is prepared in the same basic manner—by first sautéing it in oil or butter and then adding broth, a ladleful at a time, and stirring continuously until the rice is cooked (about 20 minutes) and all the liquid has been absorbed. This basic risotto can be flavored using a variety of ingredients, such as butter, cheese, herbs, vegetables, meat, or fish. The finest Arborio rice comes from the Piedmont region in northern Italy.

7. **Yellow Onions.** These common, all-purpose onions are a staple when making stocks, sauces, and broths. Though harsh if eaten raw, they become rich and sweet when cooked.

8. **Garlic.** Nothing can substitute for the flavor of fresh garlic. Keep the bulbs intact and chop only what you will be using in your recipe, for once minced, garlic will begin to discolor and lose flavor. Store garlic bulbs in an open container in a cool, dry place in your pantry, where they will keep for up to 3 months. The recipes in this book all call for fresh garlic, which I consider infinitely better than the jarred product, or the garlic powder, found in supermarkets.

10. Wine. You will use wine constantly in sauté, especially white wine. So what type should you keep on hand? Obviously, you do not want to cook with a $200 vintage, but you shouldn't use jug wine, either. Use any good table wine, such as a Chianti or a cabernet for a red, and a moderately priced Chardonnay or Pinot Grigio for a white. Go to your local liquor store or wine shop and ask for help in making your selection. This also applies to choosing a sherry or Marsala wine for cooking. Don't buy the cooking sherry or Marsala sold in the supermarket. Liquor stores will offer moderately priced bottles larger than what you will find in the supermarket, so you end up with a far better product for less money.

11. Flour. All-purpose, unbleached white flour that has not been chemically whitened is good for a wide range of uses, including dredging and additions to sauces. Store it in an airtight container, in a cool dry place in the pantry, away from light. It will keep for up to six months.

12. Polenta. Polenta, a type of cornmeal, is a grainy yellow flour made from ground maize. It is incredibly versatile. Like risotto, it takes about 20 minutes to cook, although there are quick-cooking varieties on the market that can be prepared in 5 minutes. When boiled, it retains a dense texture, similar to the thickness of oatmeal, and can be served plain, flavored with butter and cheese, or with vegetables, sausage, game, or other meats. When cold, it quickly hardens and can be cut into pieces and fried or grilled. At the restaurant, I also use uncooked polenta instead of breadcrumbs as a coating for calamari.

13. Breadcrumbs. Breadcrumbs add a crispy coating to pan-fried meats and fish. You can make your own breadcrumbs from slightly stale bread using a hand-held box grater, or by putting pieces of the bread though a food processor. Breadcrumbs are also readily available in any supermarket. Either way, use unseasoned breadcrumbs. The seasonings found in commercially produced breadcrumbs may clash with the seasonings in the dishes you are preparing.

I

SAUTÉED appetizers

⊠

HAVE YOU EVER noticed how many people come away from a dinner party or a restaurant dinner saying that they enjoyed the appetizers more than the entrées? Why? Is it because the appetizers are usually far more interesting than the main course? Is it because the smaller portions make it possible for them to sample a larger variety of different foods? Both, I think.

As a chef preparing for a meal service, I rarely sit down for a full meal. Instead, I usually have small tastes of many dishes, sauces, and accompaniments. It's a lot of fun to eat that way.

The recipes in this chapter are a sampling of appetizers that I have served thousands of times at my restaurant and at catering parties.

SAUTÉED SPINACH
WITH GORGONZOLA

T HIS IS A simple appetizer that can be made in 3 minutes or less. Don't let the speed and simplicity fool you into thinking that the finished dish is anything less than delicious. It's fully worthy as a first course or as a side dish to even the loftiest of meals. Use either bagged or bulk spinach, crinkled or smooth. Keep in mind, however, that spinach cooks down to almost nothing, so always buy and use more than you'll think you need. I recommend a standard 10-ounce bag for 2 people. Be sure the oil is very hot oil to prevent the spinach from absorbing too much oil.

makes 4 servings

4 to 5 tablespoons extra virgin olive oil

Pinch of red pepper flakes

2 bags (10 ounces each) fresh spinach leaves

I small clove garlic, minced

2 to 3 tablespoons chicken broth

Salt and freshly ground black pepper to taste

2 to 3 tablespoons Gorgonzola cheese

Put the olive oil and red pepper flakes in a large skillet over high heat for about 30 seconds, until the oil is hot but not smoking. Cook the spinach for about 1 minute, until it begins to wilt. Sauté the garlic for about 15 seconds, or just until it begins to brown. Add the chicken broth, and cook for 1 minute more. Season with the salt and pepper, transfer to a warm platter, and top the spinach with the Gorgonzola.

BRUSCHETTA WITH TOMATOES, FRESH MOZZARELLA, BASIL, AND KALAMATA OLIVES

ALTHOUGH BRUSCHETTA CAN be found on chic restaurant menus around the country, the classic is humble—a slice of grilled, toasted, or broiled Italian bread, rubbed with garlic and topped with diced fresh tomatoes and a bit of olive oil. My restaurant features a bruschetta (pronounced brus-*ket*-a) of the day. We've topped the bread with wild mushrooms, grilled chicken and asparagus, artichokes, olives, melted Asiago cheese—wherever our imagination leads. See where yours leads. Here's one of my favorites.

makes 4 servings

4 slices (each ¼-inch thick) crusty bread

1 clove garlic, halved

2 tablespoons extra virgin olive oil

½ small clove garlic, minced

2 plum tomatoes, chopped

¼ cup kalamata olives, pitted and halved

6 basil leaves, finely chopped

½ pound fresh mozzarella, cut in medium dice

Salt and freshly ground black pepper to taste

Brown the bread slices on a grill or under the broiler, taking care not to let the bread burn. Rub a cut surface of the halved garlic clove over each slice. Meanwhile, place a small sauté pan with the olive oil and minced garlic over high heat for about 30 seconds, or just until the garlic begins to turn golden brown. Place the chopped tomato in the hot oil, cook for 1 minute, turn off the heat, and add the olives, basil, and diced mozzarella. Stir and season with salt and pepper. Top each slice with a portion of the pan mixture.

NOTE: This recipe can easily be doubled or tripled.

MUSSELS AND SCALLOPS
IN A BALSAMIC WINE SAUCE

THOUGH I MAKE this dish with mussels and scallops, you could use shrimp, calamari, clams, or any firm fish that will hold its shape. This dish showcases the strong flavor of the balsamic vinegar, and a little bit goes a long way toward flavoring a dish. Pair it with the White Wine Sauce to give it a thick, creamy texture.

makes 4 servings

2 to 3 tablespoons extra virgin olive oil

Pinch of red pepper flakes

1 dozen large sea scallops

1 medium clove garlic, minced

2 dozen mussels

¼ cup fish broth

¼ cup White Wine Sauce (page 222)

3 tablespoons high-quality balsamic vinegar

1 teaspoon heavy cream (optional)

1 tablespoon Italian (flat-leaf) parsley, stems removed and chopped

Salt and freshly ground black pepper to taste

Put the olive oil and red pepper flakes in a large sauté pan over high heat for about 30 seconds, until the oil is hot but not smoking. Cook the scallops in the hot oil for about 1 minute, or until the bottoms of the scallops are brown. Turn the scallops and brown on the second side. Cook for about 1 minute more, add the garlic, and cook for a few seconds, until the garlic just begins to turn golden brown. Cook the mussels for about 1 minute or until they start to open.

Add the fish broth, White Wine Sauce, and balsamic vinegar, and cook until the scallops are opaque, the mussels fully open and opaque, and the sauce has a thick, creamy texture. Add the cream, transfer the mixture to a serving bowl, and sprinkle with the parsley. Season with salt and pepper.

NOTE: If you do not have any premade White Wine Sauce, make it right in the sauté pan. Add 1 tablespoon of flour to the pan juices, stir with a wire whisk to make a roux, add about 2 tablespoons of white wine, and stir. Slowly add ¼ to ⅓ cup of fish broth and continue to stir until you have a smooth sauce.

heavy cream

SOMEWHERE ALONG THE way, we got the idea that in order to eat healthfully, we had to completely avoid sweets, red meat, butter, cream, etc.—in other words, all of the good stuff. Isn't it also true that whatever we deny ourselves is exactly what we crave? I've always believed in denying myself nothing—well, almost nothing. Indulging is always a matter of degree and balance. This is why I finish many of my recipes with heavy cream, rather than use it as a main ingredient. One or 2 tablespoons of heavy cream divided among 4 servings is a paltry amount, not enough to even waste an ounce of guilt, yet the gain in texture and perceived richness is significant. A frequent use: as a "finish" for sauces and soups. The tiny amount of cream lightens the color and adds a rich smoothness to these liquids.

MANILA CLAMS OREGANATO

MANILA CLAMS ARE small, sometimes barely an inch in diameter, so they open quickly when sautéed. They're sweet, distinctively flavorful, and are a favorite of chefs across the country. Although they are also called Japanese clams, they are farmed off the Pacific coast of the United States but are not native to the region. For the best flavor, try to use them the same day you buy them, but if you must store them remember that they are alive and must breathe. Refrigerate them for a day or two in a shallow bowl with ice over them. (Refresh the ice as it melts.)

makes 4 servings

12 slices (each ¼-inch thick) hard-crusted baguette

1 clove garlic, halved

3 to 4 tablespoons extra virgin olive oil

Pinch of red pepper flakes

½ medium clove garlic, minced

2 dozen Manila clams (or the smallest clams you can find)

¼ cup dry white wine

¼ cup fish broth or clam juice

1 teaspoon chopped fresh oregano or ½ teaspoon dried

1 teaspoon Italian (flat-leaf) parsley, stems removed and chopped

Freshly ground black pepper to taste

Brown the baguette slices on a grill or under the broiler, taking care not to let the bread burn. Rub each slice with a cut surface of the halved garlic clove. Drizzle a total of about 1 tablespoon of the olive oil over the bread slices.

Meanwhile, put the remaining olive oil, red pepper flakes, and minced garlic in a medium sauté pan over high heat for about 30 seconds, or just until the garlic begins to brown. Sauté the clams in the hot oil for 1 minute. Add the wine and reduce for 1 minute, then the fish broth or clam juice and reduce for another 1 to 2 minutes, until all the clams have opened and the liquid has thickened. Add the oregano and parsley, transfer the mixture to a large serving bowl, top with the bread, and season with the black pepper.

TWO-MINUTE CALAMARI WITH PINE NUTS, TOMATOES, AND SCALLIONS

I LOVE FRIED calamari, so I usually order it in restaurants, even though I'm often disappointed with what I get. Calamari must be cooked at a high temperature for a short time or at medium temperature for a longer time. Unfortunately, local fire codes won't allow my restaurant (a wooden building of 1830s vintage) to have a deep fryer. What's a chef to do when she can't put her own favorite on her restaurant menu? That's right: I sauté it. Sauté is fast and can be done over high heat, so it's a perfect way to cook calamari. Frankly, this combination of calamari, sweet scallions, crunchy pine nuts, and fresh tomatoes makes fried calamari look, well, boring. Here's calamari like you've never had it before.

makes 4 servings

¼ cup extra virgin olive oil

Pinch of red pepper flakes

1 small clove garlic, minced

1 pound calamari tubes, cut in ½-inch rings

2 plum tomatoes, coarsely diced

¼ cup dry white wine

¼ cup fish broth

¼ cup White Wine Sauce (page 222)

2 fresh scallions, halved lengthwise and coarsely diced

Salt and freshly ground black pepper to taste

¼ cup pine nuts

1 tablespoon Italian (flat-leaf) parsley, stems removed and chopped

Put the olive oil, red pepper flakes, and garlic in a medium sauté pan over high heat for about 30 seconds, or just until the garlic begins to brown. Sauté the calamari for 1 minute. Add the tomatoes, wine, fish broth, White Wine Sauce, and scallions, and cook for 1 minute more, or until the sauce begins to boil. Remove from the heat, and test a piece of calamari for doneness. It should be opaque and tender. If not, cook it a little longer. Season with salt and pepper, transfer to a large bowl, add the pine nuts, sprinkle with the parsley, and adjust the seasonings if desired.

37

BREADED SMOKED MOZZARELLA IN A WHITE WINE SAUCE WITH ARUGULA

M OZZARELLA, WHICH WE all know and love, takes on a whole new quality when smoked. It becomes firmer and denser, and, when sliced into medallions, breaded, and sautéed, the cheese holds its shape while lightly melting. The neutral taste of the White Wine Sauce tones down the strong flavor of the cheese but still allows the smoky flavor to infuse the sauce. Serving this over green, peppery arugula leaves and slices of sweet red tomatoes results in a sophisticated yet simple appetizer in which intense flavors result in a harmonious dish that's pleasing to the eye and interesting to the palate.

makes 2 servings

½ pound smoked mozzarella, cut in about 6 slices, each ¼-inch thick

2 eggs, beaten with a splash of water

½ cup breadcrumbs

3 to 4 tablespoons extra virgin olive oil

1 medium clove garlic, minced

2 to 3 tablespoons dry white wine

½ cup White Wine Sauce (page 222)

¼ cup chicken broth

Salt and freshly ground black pepper to taste

1 large tomato, cut in about 6 slices, each ¼ inch thick (see note)

1 tablespoon Italian (flat-leaf) parsley, stems removed and chopped

10 fresh arugula leaves

Dip each mozzarella slice in the beaten egg, then in the breadcrumbs. Pat to be sure that the breadcrumbs adhere, and set them on a dish.

Put the olive oil in a large skillet over high heat for about 30 seconds, until the oil is hot but not smoking. Place the mozzarella slices in the hot oil and cook for about 30 seconds, until the coated cheese pieces are golden brown. Turn the pieces, and cook for another minute, or until the second sides brown. Add the garlic and cook for a few seconds, just until the garlic begins to brown. Add the wine and cook for about 30 seconds. Add the White Wine Sauce and the chicken broth, and continue to cook, letting the liquid thicken, for another minute, until the sauce begins to boil. Remove from the heat and season with the salt and pepper.

To serve, arrange each plate with half the arugula in a clockwise fashion, top with three tomato slices and three mozzarella pieces, and sprinkle with parsley to garnish, if desired, with a red pepper or slice of radicchio.

NOTE: If regular tomatoes are of poor quality, you may substitute plum tomatoes.

WILD MUSHROOMS with SUN-DRIED TOMATOES and SHERRY

A T BISCOTTI, WE serve so many of these appetizers, either plain or over risotto or polenta, that I wanted to rename the restaurant The Wild Mushroom Café. I was talked out of it. But I'll never be talked out of this dish. I use a combination of three wild mushrooms—portabellos, cremino (baby portabellos), and shiitakes, although any combination of wild mushrooms will do. All of them are widely available in supermarkets.

makes 4 servings

2 to 3 tablespoons extra virgin olive oil

Pinch of red pepper flakes

2 large portabello mushrooms, stems removed and cut in $1/4$-inch slices (see note)

12 cremino mushrooms, quartered (see note)

12 shiitake mushrooms, stems removed, sliced in halves or thirds (see note)

1 medium clove garlic, minced

2 to 3 tablespoons sherry

$1/4$ cup White Wine Sauce (page 222)

$1/4$ cup Marinara Sauce (page 224)

$1/4$ cup dry-packed sun-dried tomatoes, slivered

$1/2$ cup chicken broth

Salt and freshly ground black pepper to taste

1 tablespoon Italian (flat-leaf) parsley, stems removed and chopped

Put the olive oil and red pepper flakes in a large skillet over high heat for about 30 seconds, until the oil is hot but not smoking. Cook the mushrooms in the hot oil for

2 to 3 minutes, or until they begin to soften. Cook the garlic for about 30 seconds, just until it begins to brown, then deglaze the pan with the sherry by cooking for 1 minute more. Add the White Wine Sauce, Marinara Sauce, sun-dried tomatoes, and chicken broth, and cook for 2 to 3 minutes. If the sauce is too thick, add a bit more chicken broth and remove from heat. Season with the salt and pepper. Place on a decorative platter and sprinkle with the parsley.

NOTE: As long as the approximate total weight of the mushrooms is maintained, you may vary the amount of the three varieties.

41

RISOTTO ZUCCHINI CAKES

MY MOTHER USED to make these cakes with just the risotto. They were so good that she had to hide them so they wouldn't disappear before she got them to the table. The creaminess of the risotto makes it easy to shape them into cakes. The zucchini makes a good treat even better. I've also made these with bits of salmon. Try the recipe below, then come up with your own variations. You can easily double or triple this recipe—and can prepare the cakes the day before—for perfect make-ahead appetizers for a buffet or dinner party.

makes 4 servings

1 cup Arborio rice, cooked according to package directions

1 medium egg, beaten

2 small to medium zucchini, shredded

1 medium clove garlic, minced

½ teaspoon salt

1 tablespoon Italian (flat-leaf) parsley, stems removed and chopped

Freshly ground black pepper to taste

½ cup breadcrumbs

½ cup seasoned flour, for dredging

6 to 7 tablespoons olive oil

To make the risotto, combine the rice, egg, zucchini, garlic, salt, parsley, and black pepper in a large bowl. The mixture should be sticky. Shape into 2-inch balls, flatten each into a small cake, and make the edges of the circles even. Place the breadcrumbs in a second bowl and the flour in a third. Coat each risotto cake with breadcrumbs, then dredge in flour. Set aside.

Put the olive oil in a large skillet over high heat for about 60 seconds, until the oil is hot but not smoking. Cook 4 or 5 cakes in the hot oil for about 1 minute on each side, until golden brown. Remove the cakes and place them on paper towels to absorb any excess oil. Repeat until all the cakes are cooked. Place on a serving platter.

They are best served warm or at room temperature. If you make them in advance, store them in an oblong pan in the refrigerator with paper towels between each layer to absorb any excess oil. Before serving, remove the paper towels and reheat them in a 350°F oven for 10 to 15 minutes, or until they are just warm.

zucchini delicacy

ZUCCHINI PRODUCE AN edible blossom that's a great Italian delicacy. Growing up, my parents used to make a batter, much like a tempura batter, dip the blossoms in it and then fry them. They are heavenly. Zucchini blossoms are the first "fruits" of the summer garden, so I celebrate their arrival by frying them or sautéing them in a sauce. If you can find zucchini blossoms, rinse them, slice them in half, and add them to a tomato sauce (after you add the zucchini and before you add the tomatoes). Zucchini, like eggplant, are highly versatile. They can be baked, grilled, fried, sautéed, shredded, and stuffed.

EGGS AND PEPPERS

THIS IS A delicious, classic "peasant" dish from my region of Calabria. I'm guessing that when meat and fish were scarce, eggs with peppers and a piece of crusty bread were usually available for a tasty, low-cost meal. We may be able to afford more now, but eggs and peppers still make a tasty dish. The dish will work with bell peppers, but I think the green ones are too heavy, the red and yellow ones too sweet. It's best made with Italian frying peppers lighter in color and weight, thinner, and more elongated, much like a sweet chile pepper. In fact, I think a mild chile pepper would be better than a bell pepper. Italian frying peppers are available in most supermarkets or farmers' markets in the Northeast, and, I imagine, anywhere that has a large Italian population. If you can't find them, go for the bell peppers (look for firm, unwrinkled, shiny skins). This dish is best made in a nonstick pan.

makes 4 servings

3 to 4 tablespoons extra virgin olive oil

2 to 3 Italian frying peppers, cut into ¼-inch slices

1 small clove garlic, minced

8 eggs, beaten and seasoned with salt and freshly ground black pepper to taste

1 tablespoon Italian (flat-leaf) parsley, stems removed and chopped

Put the oil in a large, nonstick skillet over high heat for about 30 seconds and cook the peppers in the hot oil for 1 to 2 minutes, or until the peppers have softened. Stir occasionally to prevent them from burning. Cook the garlic for about 15 seconds, just until it starts to turn golden, then reduce the heat. Add the eggs and turn, as you would when making scrambled eggs, until they are cooked, about 2 minutes. Remove from the heat, place on a warm platter, and sprinkle with fresh chopped parsley.

SAUTÉED DICED EGGPLANT
AND TOMATOES

I F YOU LOVE eggplant, you'll love this quick, delicious sauté. (Vegetarians would be hard-pressed to find another dish this easy and this good.) The juices from the fresh tomatoes and the oil combine to make a delicious sauce that perfectly complements the flavorful eggplant. Like the preceding dish of eggs and peppers, this recipe demonstrates the resourcefulness, simplicity, and brilliance of Italian "peasant" food. Even today, when most families in southern Italy and Sicily can afford meat, the eggplant, once a popular substitute, still plays an important role. Serve this as an appetizer, a sauce for pasta or pizza, a side vegetable for meat or fish, or even a topping for bruschetta. Like the eggplant itself, this is a versatile dish.

makes 4 servings

4 to 5 tablespoons extra virgin olive oil

I firm, medium eggplant, unpeeled, center core removed, cut in medium dice

½ small clove garlic, minced

2 plum tomatoes, diced

Salt and freshly ground black pepper to taste

3 fresh basil leaves, sliced

Put the oil in a large skillet over high heat for about 30 seconds, or until the oil is hot but not smoking. Cook the diced eggplant in the hot oil until golden brown on all sides, about 2 minutes. Cook the garlic for about 15 seconds, or just until the garlic begins to brown, then add the tomatoes and cook for about 30 seconds more, until the tomatoes are softened but still firm.

Remove from the heat, season with salt and pepper, and transfer the mixture to a serving platter. Top with the basil slices.

SHRIMP SCAMPI
WITH SPINACH

S HRIMP SCAMPI, THOUGH we see it on many Italian menus, is a misnomer. "Scampi" actually refers to a type of shrimp, usually small to medium, so "shrimp scampi" actually means "shrimp shrimp." I'll keep the misnomer going, because shrimp sautéed in oil or butter, garlic, and lemon or wine has become so widely known as shrimp scampi. Whatever it's called, it's quick, flavorful, and versatile—wonderful served alone, over pasta, or even as a sauce over another fish, such as tuna or sea bass. The pairing of shrimp and spinach in this recipe's easy oil-garlic-wine sauce brings together two ingredients that I would sauté the same way were I to cook each of them alone. Together, they are simply marvelous.

**makes 2 servings as an entrée or
4 servings as a side dish or an appetizer**

4 to 5 tablespoons extra virgin olive oil

Pinch of red pepper flakes

12 medium shrimp, shells removed, cleaned and deveined

½ small clove garlic, minced

2 to 3 tablespoons dry white wine

1 bag (10 ounces) fresh spinach

1 tablespoon Italian (flat-leaf) parsley, stems removed and chopped

Salt and freshly ground black pepper to taste

Put the oil and red pepper flakes in a large skillet over high heat for about 30 seconds, until the oil is hot but not smoking. Cook the shrimp until they begin to turn pink on one side, about 1 minute. Turn the shrimp so they cook on the other side and sauté the garlic for about 15 seconds, until it starts to turn golden. Add the wine and cook for about 30 seconds. Cook the spinach for about 1 minute, until the leaves begin to wilt and the shrimp are completely pink on the outside and opaque on the inside. Sprinkle with the parsley. Remove from the heat, season with salt and pepper, and transfer to a warm serving platter.

cooking shrimp

IT'S SO EASY to overcook shrimp and make them rubbery. Just a few seconds will do it. To avoid that, slightly undercook the shrimp. Even after the shrimp come off the heat, they'll continue to cook in the hot sauce, so by the time the shrimp get to the table, they'll be perfect. Shrimp are cooked when they're pink on the outside and opaque on the inside. This usually takes about 3 minutes.

2

SAUTÉED poultry

ASK MEAT LOVERS which meat they eat the most and the answer will surely be chicken. The same holds true at my restaurant, Biscotti. Hands down, chicken is the No. 1 best seller. It seems we can never have enough interesting ways to cook and eat it. Some likely reasons: Chicken is naturally low in fat, delicious, and very versatile. The variations for sautéing chicken are almost endless. In this chapter, I'll give you recipes for some of the best-selling dishes at the restaurant, as well as some of my personal favorites.

Some Things You Should Know

Chicken must be cooked thoroughly, with all pieces reaching an internal temperature of 150°F to 160°F. Cutting chicken into thin, small, uniform pieces—as it's done for sauté—will reduce the cooking time while still ensuring doneness. It also makes it unnecessary to check the meat's internal temperature. You can tell the pieces are done when they are no longer translucent, and are opaque throughout, with no pink spots visible.

Because most of the chicken recipes in this chapter call for thin pieces, you may find it convenient to butterfly the breasts. To butterfly something means to cut it almost all the way through, without cutting it into two pieces—so that it spreads out and lies flat, like butterfly wings. Chicken breasts become twice as wide and half as thick, resulting in fast, even cooking. Note that one complete chicken breast has *two* halves—half a breast is what is generally considered a piece of chicken suitable for one diner.

Chicken, like most other meat, is sold in grades, and each grade has specific FDA standards. **Grade A** chicken has met FDA standards and is the grade most readily available to consumers. **Natural** means that the chicken contains no artificial ingredients. **Free-range** indicates that the chicken was raised with access to the outdoors. **Organic** means that the producer has adhered to strict standards and certification, ensuring that the chickens have been in free-range conditions, have been given only organic feed, and have not been injected with any hormones or antibiotics.

Many of the chicken recipes that I've written to be served with pasta could also be served alone or with potatoes or risotto.

Cook chicken with any combination of your favorite ingredients. Some combinations will work better than others, but you'll never know until you try.

CHICKEN WITH ZUCCHINI AND TOMATOES OVER SPAGHETTI

T HOUGH THIS RECIPE is always delicious, it is truly unforgettable in the summer when zucchini and tomatoes come right out of the garden. If you don't have a garden, your local supermarket or farmer's market is sure to have plenty of zucchini, year-round. Zucchini, a member of the squash family, can grow very large, but they are most tender, and less seedy, if they are harvested when they are no more than 8 inches long. For vegetarians, make this recipe minus the chicken. It's still wonderful.

makes 4 servings

1 pound spaghetti or other long pasta, such as linguine

¼ cup extra virgin olive oil

Pinch of red pepper flakes

2 large chicken breasts, split, each piece dredged in seasoned flour and cut into 3 or 4 strips

2 medium zucchini, cut into ¼-inch-thick circular slices

1 medium clove garlic, minced

4 plum tomatoes, cut in medium dice

3 to 4 tablespoons dry white wine

¼ cup White Wine Sauce (page 222)

¼ cup chicken broth

2 to 3 tablespoons heavy cream (optional)

Salt and freshly ground black pepper to taste

1 tablespoon Italian (flat-leaf) parsley, stems removed and chopped

Cook the pasta according to package directions in a large pot of salted, boiling water.

While the pasta cooks, put the olive oil and red pepper flakes in a large sauté pan over high heat for about 1 minute, until the oil is hot but not smoking. Sauté the chicken strips in the hot oil for 1 to 2 minutes on each side, until the chicken is golden brown. Sauté the zucchini slices until they are golden brown and slightly softened but still firm, about 1 minute. Cook the garlic and stir for about 30 seconds, or just until the garlic begins to brown. Add the tomatoes and cook for another minute. Deglaze the pan with the wine, add the White Wine Sauce and the chicken broth, and cook for 1 to 2 minutes more, until the sauce begins to boil. Reduce the heat to low, stir in the cream, and simmer for about 1 more minute, until the sauce thickens. Remove from the heat and season with the salt and pepper.

To serve, drain the pasta, place it in a large serving bowl, and toss with half the liquid part of the sauce. Put the pasta on individual serving plates and top each portion with some additional sauce and the solid ingredients in the pan. Sprinkle with the parsley.

deglazing

WHEN YOU MAKE a sauce in a sauté pan, bits of various ingredients cling to the bottom of the skillet. These bits are very flavorful and should be released into the sauce. The process of doing that is called deglazing. Usually it's done by adding an acidic liquid like wine or lemon juice to the hot contents of the pan.

CHICKEN WITH SUN-DRIED TOMATO PESTO SAUCE OVER PENNE

TRADITIONAL PESTO, MADE with basil, garlic, oil, pine nuts, and Parmesan, has become a staple sauce for pasta now that the ingredients have become readily available. Many supermarkets now stock ready-made pesto sauce, usually next to their fresh pasta, but sun-dried tomatoes can serve as the foundation to a delicious alternative. The concentrated tomato flavor works wonderfully with the basil and the parsley. I'm sure you'll want to use this pesto in omelets and salads or as a spread. In this recipe, it adds intensity to the chicken and coats the ridges in the penne so that each bit is bursting with flavor.

makes 4 servings

1 pound penne rigate

3 tablespoons extra virgin olive oil

2 large chicken breasts, split, each piece cut into 3 or 4 strips and dredged in seasoned flour

1 medium clove garlic, minced

1 cup Sun-Dried Tomato Pesto Sauce (recipe follows)

3 to 4 tablespoons sherry

1/2 cup chicken broth

1/4 cup heavy cream (optional)

Salt and freshly ground black pepper to taste

1 tablespoon Italian (flat-leaf) parsley, stems removed and chopped

4 large basil leaves, for garnish

Cook the pasta according to package directions in a large pot of salted, boiling water.

While the pasta cooks, put the olive oil in a large skillet over medium heat for about 1 minute and lightly brown the chicken pieces in the hot oil for about 1 minute on each side. Cook the garlic for about 30 seconds, just until it begins to brown. Add the Sun-Dried Tomato Pesto Sauce, stir, and deglaze the pan with the sherry, stir, and cook for about 1 minute more. Add the chicken broth, stir and cook for about 1 minute until the sauce begins to boil. Stir in the cream, reduce the heat to low, and cook for about 1 minute, until the sauce thickens. (If the sauce is too thick, add a bit more chicken broth.) Remove from the heat and season with the salt and pepper.

To serve, drain the pasta, place it in a large serving bowl, and toss with half the liquid part of the sauce. Put the pasta on individual serving plates, and top each portion with some additional sauce liquid and the solid ingredients in the pan. Sprinkle with parsley and garnish with basil.

SUN-DRIED TOMATO PESTO SAUCE

Makes about 3 cups

2 cups dry-packed sun-dried tomatoes

½ cup fresh basil leaves

½ cup Italian (flat-leaf) parsley, stems removed

½ cup pine nuts

¼ cup Parmesan cheese, grated

1 cup extra virgin olive oil

1 cup chicken broth

Salt and freshly ground black pepper to taste

Put the tomatoes, basil, parsley, pine nuts, and Parmesan in the workbowl of a food processor, and pulse until they are coarsely chopped. Slowly add the oil and broth, and continue to pulse until the mixture forms a grainy paste. Season with salt and pepper. Use 1 cup as directed in previous recipe, and use the remainder to coat chicken in other dishes, in omelets, or as a spread.

LINGUINE WITH CHICKEN, ASPARAGUS, BACON, AND SUN-DRIED TOMATOES

T HIS RECIPE IS a personal favorite and a favorite of many staffers at Biscotti. Maybe it's because the sun-dried tomatoes and bacon make this dish intense in flavor and color, perfectly complementing the light flavor and color of the asparagus, chicken, and sauce. The result is a dish more pleasing than the sum of its parts. An important part of sauté, and all cooking, is knowing what ingredients work well together. I devised this particular dish using pure instinct. Though this is a trait common to naturally good cooks, it's an ability that can be developed even by the most "by-the-book" cooks. Just trust your ideas and inspirations. If something you've concocted doesn't taste good, try again with other ingredients. The point is, don't be afraid to experiment.

makes 4 servings

1 pound linguine

¼ cup extra virgin olive oil

Pinch of red pepper flakes

2 large boneless chicken breasts, split, cut in a total of 12 to 16 strips, and dredged in seasoned flour

12 stalks fresh asparagus, trimmed and parboiled so as to still be firm, halved lengthwise if thick

3 medium cloves garlic, minced

2 to 3 tablespoons white wine

1 cup White Wine Sauce (page 222)

½ cup chicken broth

¼ cup dry-packed sun-dried tomatoes, cut into thin strips

3 tablespoons heavy cream

Salt and freshly ground black pepper to taste

6 slices bacon, cooked crisp, drained, and broken into small pieces

1 tablespoon Italian (flat-leaf) parsley, stems removed and chopped

Cook the pasta according to package directions in a large pot of salted, boiling water.

While the pasta cooks, put the olive oil and red pepper flakes in a large sauté pan over high heat for 1 minute. Sauté the chicken for 1 to 2 minutes per side, or until it turns opaque and golden brown. Cook the asparagus and garlic for 30 seconds, or just until the garlic begins to brown. Deglaze the pan by adding the wine, stir, and cook for 1 minute more. Add the White Wine Sauce, chicken broth, and sun-dried tomatoes, and cook for about 2 minutes, until the sauce begins to boil. Add the cream, stir, reduce heat to low, and simmer for about 1 minute, until the sauce thickens. Remove from the heat and season with the salt and pepper.

To serve, drain the pasta and toss it in a large serving bowl with half of the liquid part of the sauce. Place the pasta on individual serving plates and top each portion with some additional sauce and the chicken, asparagus, and sun-dried tomatoes. Sprinkle with the bacon and parsley.

NOTE: If necessary, the bacon pieces can be warmed in a microwave oven for a few seconds.

Venus and Mars

OVER THE YEARS, I've noticed some pronounced gender differences in my restaurant, among both staffers and customers. In general, men tend to prefer heavier, red sauces, while women tend to prefer white sauces that are perceived as lighter (even though that's not necessarily true). For example, the favorite dish of the Biscotti women is Linguine with Chicken, Asparagus, Bacon, and Sun-Dried Tomatoes. I've also noticed the same gender differences in wine. Men seem to prefer reds (especially cabernets), while women prefer white wines. My own children also seem to follow gender differences in their choices. My daughter's favorite sauce is alfredo, my son's, tomato and pesto.

mushrooms

WHEN SELECTING MUSHROOMS, look for firm, smooth, unblemished caps that aren't limp, wrinkled, or moldy, and for stems that are neither gray nor dried out (indications that they are old). Store mushrooms in a cardboard box or brown paper bag in the refrigerator, never in plastic (which would make them slimy and moldy). Mushrooms absorb liquid easily, so never rinse them under water. Instead, clean them by gently wiping away any dirt with a damp cloth.

CHICKEN MARSALA
WITH WILD MUSHROOMS

S OME PEOPLE SAY you should never fool with a classic, but I disagree. Chicken Marsala is considered a classic Italian dish, which explains its appearance on so many menus, from pizzerias to five-star restaurants. Like any dish, it can be made poorly by chefs willing to use canned mushrooms and cheap wine, or it can be raised to a whole new level with fresh wild mushrooms and a good Marsala wine. My recipe goes even one step further: Besides wild mushrooms, I add sun-dried tomatoes and a bit of white wine sauce. This adds a rich creaminess to the dish. A hint of marinara sauce also adds color and extra flavor. This dish is a Biscotti classic. Serve it with some risotto on the side.

makes 4 servings

½ cup extra virgin olive oil

Pinch of red pepper flakes

2 large boneless chicken breasts, split, each piece cut horizontally into 3 thin slices (resulting in 12 thin slices) and dredged in seasoned flour

1 large clove garlic, minced

⅓ cup marsala wine

2 large portabello mushrooms, stems removed and cut in ¼-inch slices (see note)

12 cremino mushrooms, quartered (see note)

12 shiitake mushrooms, stems removed and sliced in half or thirds (see note)

½ pound sun-dried tomatoes, sliced

½ cup chicken broth

½ cup White Wine Sauce (page 222) (see note)

½ cup Marinara Sauce (page 224)

Salt and freshly ground black pepper to taste

1 tablespoon Italian (flat-leaf) parsley, stems removed and chopped

Put about 2 tablespoons of the olive oil and some red pepper flakes in a large sauté pan over high heat for about 1 minute, until the oil is hot but not smoking. Cook half the chicken for 1 to 2 minutes per side, or until the meat turns opaque and golden brown. Keep the chicken warm while you cook the second batch, first heating another 2 tablespoons of oil and some pepper flakes. Remove the chicken from the pan, and keep it warm, along with the first batch.

In the same pan, still over high heat, heat the remaining olive oil, more pepper flakes, the garlic, and half the marsala for 30 seconds, until the oil is hot but not smoking. Cook the mushrooms and the sun-dried tomatoes in the hot oil for about 2 minutes, until the mushrooms begin to soften. Add the remaining marsala, cook for 1 minute more, and add the chicken broth, White Wine Sauce, and Marinara Sauce.

Return the chicken to the pan, lower the heat to medium, and cook for 3 to 4 minutes until the chicken is cooked thoroughly. Simmer the sauce for about 1 minute to get a thick, rich gravy. If it's too thick, add a bit more broth. Season with salt and pepper.

To serve, place chicken pieces on serving plates and top with the mushrooms, sun-dried tomatoes, and sauce. Sprinkle with the parsley.

NOTE: As long as the total approximate weight of the mushrooms is maintained, you may vary the amount of the three varieties.

NOTE: If you don't have White Wine Sauce on hand, make some right in the pan. Set the mushrooms to one side after you've softened them, add about 2 tablespoons of flour to the mushroom juices, and whisk together to make a quick paste. Add 2 to 3 tablespoons of white wine and ½ cup of chicken broth to make gravy. Cook for 1 to 2 minutes to reduce and thicken the sauce, then return the chicken to the pan and proceed. Adjust the thickness of the sauce by adding more chicken broth, if needed.

LEMON CHICKEN WITH ARTICHOKE HEARTS AND RED PEPPERS IN A WHITE WINE SAUCE

W HEN DEMONSTRATING HOW to make my white wine sauce in my cooking classes, I always make this dish because it perfectly illustrates how the individual flavors of the sautéed ingredients come through the white wine sauce, giving it a distinctive, yet never overpowering flavor. Besides, this is a beautiful as well as an unforgettably delicious dish.

makes 4 servings

4 to 5 tablespoons extra virgin olive oil

2 large boneless chicken breasts, split, each piece cut horizontally into 3 thin slices (resulting in 12 thin slices) and dredged in seasoned flour

1 medium clove garlic, minced

$\frac{1}{4}$ cup white wine

2 red bell peppers, cut in $\frac{1}{4}$-inch strips

1 cup canned artichoke hearts, drained, sliced in half or quarters, depending on size (see note)

1 cup White Wine Sauce (page 222)

Juice of 2 lemons

3 to 4 tablespoons heavy cream (optional)

Salt and freshly ground black pepper to taste

1 tablespoon Italian (flat-leaf) parsley, stems removed and chopped

1 lemon, cut in $\frac{1}{4}$-inch slices (optional garnish)

12 fresh spinach leaves (optional garnish)

Put the olive oil in a large skillet over high heat for about 30 seconds, until the oil is hot but not smoking. Cook the chicken pieces, in two batches, in the hot oil for 1 to 2 minutes per side or until the meat turns opaque and golden brown. Sauté the garlic for about 30 seconds, or just until it begins to brown, then deglaze the pan with the wine, stirring with a wooden spoon.

Cook the pepper strips until they begin to soften, about 1 minute, then add the artichoke hearts and the White Wine Sauce and cook about 2 minutes, until the sauce begins to boil. Add the lemon juice and finish with the cream. Stir and reduce the heat to low, simmering for about 1 minute, until the sauce is the consistency of a cream gravy. Remove the pan from the heat and season with salt and pepper.

Place the chicken pieces on a serving platter and spoon the liquid part of the sauce over the chicken. Top with the red peppers, artichoke hearts, and parsley. Garnish, if desired, with lemon slices and spinach leaves.

NOTE: Artichokes are usually sold in 14-ounce cans that yield about 8½ ounces after draining.

CHICKEN CUTLETS WITH MOZZARELLA, TOMATOES, AND BASIL MAYONNAISE

T HIS IS A simple, no-fuss recipe that requires little cooking beyond the chicken cutlets. Make a batch of cutlets and use them in sandwiches, other salads (such as the Chicken-Pear-Arugula Salad on page 72), or the Chicken Parmesan (page 70). Combined with the ingredients in this recipe, it makes for a terrific quick lunch or light dinner.

makes 4 to 6 servings

3 medium or large eggs, beaten with a splash of water

Salt and freshly ground black pepper to taste

1 medium clove garlic, minced

1 teaspoon fresh Italian (flat-leaf) parsley, stems removed and chopped

1 cup unseasoned breadcrumbs

2 large boneless chicken breasts, split, each piece cut horizontally into 3 thin slices (resulting in 12 thin slices) and dredged in seasoned flour

½ cup extra virgin olive oil or canola oil or a combination

4 large leaves red- or green-leaf lettuce (for garnish)

2 large ripe tomatoes, cut in ¼-inch slices (use plum tomatoes if regular tomatoes are of poor quality)

1 pound fresh mozzarella, cut in ¼-inch slices

12 fresh basil leaves

½ cup Basil Mayonnaise (recipe follows)

Season the beaten eggs with the salt, pepper, garlic, and half the parsley. Put the breadcrumbs in a medium mixing bowl. Dip the chicken pieces first in the egg mixture, then in the breadcrumbs. Each piece should be coated evenly.

Put the oil in a large sauté pan for about 1 minute over medium-high heat, until the oil is hot but not smoking. Cook the chicken pieces in two batches, for about 2 minutes per side, or until the coating turns golden brown. Place the cooked pieces on paper towels to absorb any excess oil.

To serve, place a lettuce leaf on the corner of each serving plate and top with alternating slices of tomato and mozzarella. Drizzle with additional olive oil, if desired, and sprinkle with the basil and the remaining parsley. Put 2 to 3 chicken cutlets on the center of each plate and top the chicken with a dollop of the Basil Mayonnaise.

BASIL MAYONNAISE

makes 1 cup

1 medium clove garlic, whole

1 teaspoon Dijon mustard

1 medium egg yolk

¾ cup vegetable oil

Salt and freshly ground black pepper to taste

3 to 4 fresh basil leaves, rolled and cut into thin strips

Put the garlic, mustard, and egg yolk in the workbowl of a food processor and, with the blade spinning, add the oil in a slow, steady, thin stream until it is all incorporated and the mixture is thick. Pour into a bowl and season with salt and pepper. Fold in the basil strips. Use as directed in previous recipe.

CHICKEN WITH BROCCOLI RABE OVER LINGUINE

THIS SIMPLE RECIPE is easily made, start to finish, in 30 minutes. Broccoli rabe (also known in Italian as rapini or rape) is a relatively new arrival in American supermarkets. Despite its name, broccoli rabe is not at all like broccoli. Broccoli rabe has a wonderfully bitter taste, is bright green and leafy, and has a long, thin stalk and small florets. Broccoli rabe is delicious when sautéed in a simple oil-garlic sauce because it needs little else to bring out its flavor. It makes a wonderful accompaniment to meat and fish, or, as in this recipe, a flavorful pasta sauce. Steam or parboil the broccoli rabe before sautéing to reduce bitterness and cut back on cooking time.

makes 4 servings

1 pound linguine (or other thin, long pasta)

1 bunch fresh broccoli rabe (see note)

$\frac{1}{2}$ cup extra virgin olive oil

Pinch of red pepper flakes

2 large chicken breasts, split, cut into a total of 12 strips and dredged
   in seasoned flour

1 medium clove garlic, minced

3 to 4 tablespoons white wine

2 to 3 tablespoons White Wine Sauce (page 222)

$\frac{1}{4}$ cup chicken broth

Salt and freshly ground black pepper to taste

1 tablespoon Italian (flat-leaf) parsley, stems removed and chopped

Cook the pasta according to package directions in a large pot of boiling, salted water.

While the pasta cooks, trim the broccoli rabe of any hard, dense, discolored stalk ends and remove any discolored, wilted leaves. If the stalks are thick, slice them in half lengthwise, then rinse. Briefly steam or parboil the rabe so that it's partially cooked but still firm.

Put the oil and red pepper flakes in a large sauté pan over medium-high heat and cook for about 1 minute, until the oil is hot but not smoking. Sauté the chicken strips in the hot oil for about 1 minute on each side, until each piece turns opaque and golden brown. Cook the broccoli rabe until it's softened but still firm. Add the garlic and cook for another 30 seconds until the garlic begins to brown.

Deglaze the pan by adding the wine, stir with a wooden spoon, and cook for about 1 minute. Add the White Wine Sauce and chicken broth, cook for 1 minute more, until the chicken is thoroughly cooked and the sauce begins to boil. Remove from the heat. Season with salt and pepper, adding a bit more broth if the sauce is too thick.

To serve, drain the pasta and toss it in a serving bowl with half of the liquid part of the sauce. Put some pasta on each dinner plate and top with the remaining sauce, chicken, and broccoli rabe. Sprinkle with the parsley.

NOTE: If you wish, substitute string beans or spinach, both of which are delicious when sautéed in an oil-garlic sauce.

on using and storing fresh herbs

I USE FRESH, flat-leaf Italian parsley, with its faint, peppery flavor, and basil, which has a sweet, faintly anise flavor, in almost all of the recipes in this book. Both are some of the world's best-loved herbs. Curly parsley has far less flavor than the flat-leaf variety and is better suited as pure garnish. Flat-leaf is good for both garnish and flavor. Never rinse parsley or basil until you are ready to use it, for the leaves (especially those of basil) will rot easily when in contact with water. As with most herbs, handle them gently. Store them in the refrigerator by snipping off the ends of the stems and placing them in a container of water, like a bouquet of flowers, until ready for use.

chicken parmesan

CHICKEN PARMESAN IS immediately recognized as Italian almost everywhere, but when I was researching the origins of Chicken Parmesan, I could not find any recipes for it in any of my Italian cookbooks or recipe indexes. So I searched the Internet. None of the recipes I found seemed Italian in origin, nor was Parmesan cheese a central ingredient. I had wondered about this before, whenever I'd ordered a Chicken Parmesan sandwich from a pizza restaurant. It always seemed to be chicken, tomato sauce, and melted mozzarella but no Parmesan, except a bit sprinkled on at the end. So where does Chicken Parmesan come from? Here's my educated guess: It was invented in America by immigrants from Southern Italy who came here in large numbers after World Wars I and II. They brought their rich culinary traditions with them, opened pizza parlors where they settled, and developed other menu items that appealed to American tastes. So wedges, heroes, hoagies, etc., were created and passed on, and, before long, items such as Chicken Parmesan became so mainstream that today they're everywhere.

CHICKEN PARMESAN

C HICKEN PARMESAN IS a simple and familiar Italian dish, yet its taste will vary greatly, depending on who prepared it and on the freshness of the ingredients. Any time you have a recipe with just a few ingredients, all of them are key and must be the best. Here, that means the freshest chicken, delicious tomato sauce, and high-quality cheeses. The success of the dish will also depend on how the chicken is breaded and cooked. Bread the chicken lightly to prevent the breading from separating later, and sauté the chicken until it is golden brown and the meat is slightly underdone, for it will continue cooking when it's baked with the sauce and the cheese.

makes 4 servings

3 medium eggs, beaten with a splash of water

Salt and freshly ground black pepper to taste

1 medium clove garlic, minced

1 teaspoon Italian (flat-leaf) parsley, stems removed and chopped

1 cup unseasoned breadcrumbs

½ cup grated Parmesan cheese

2 large boneless chicken breasts, split, each piece cut horizontally into 3 thin slices
    and dredged in seasoned flour

½ cup extra virgin olive oil, canola oil, or a combination

2 cups Marinara Sauce (page 224)

8 ounces fresh mozzarella, shredded

Season the beaten eggs with salt, pepper, garlic, and half the parsley. In another mixing bowl, combine the breadcrumbs with half the Parmesan cheese. Dip the chicken pieces first in the egg mixture, then the breadcrumbs. Be sure they're coated evenly.

Pour the oil in a large sauté pan and cook it over medium-high heat for about 1 minute. Cook the chicken pieces, in batches if necessary, for about 2 minutes on each side, or until the coating is golden brown. Put the cooked chicken pieces on paper towels to absorb any excess oil.

Add enough Marinara Sauce to cover the bottom of a 9-inch square baking pan. Add half the chicken pieces, a sprinkling of some of the remaining Parmesan and parsley, a small amount of the remaining Marinara Sauce, and about half the mozzarella. Repeat, finishing the Parmesan and the parsley, but hold off on the remaining mozzarella, which will be added during the baking. (You can assemble this up to 2 days in advance, or it can be frozen for longer.)

Bake, covered, at 350°F for approximately 15 minutes. Then sprinkle the remaining mozzarella over the top and bake for 15 minutes more, or until the center is warm and all the cheese has melted. Remove from the oven and let stand for about 10 minutes before serving.

CHICKEN-PEAR-ARUGULA SALAD
WITH SESAME POPPY DRESSING

THIS REFRESHING SALAD can be enjoyed any time of year, as good pears always seem to be plentiful, almost everywhere. The dressing is truly wonderful and can be used on any salad, or even as a marinade for chicken or fish. It is perfect combined with some of those chicken cutlets you made earlier in this chapter.

makes 2 servings

3 medium eggs, beaten with a splash of water

Salt and freshly ground black pepper to taste

1 medium clove garlic, minced

1 teaspoon Italian (flat-leaf) parsley, stems removed and chopped

1 cup unseasoned breadcrumbs

½ cup grated Parmesan cheese

2 large boneless chicken breasts, split, each piece cut horizontally into
   3 thin slices (resulting in 12 thin slices) and dredged in seasoned flour

3 to 4 tablespoons olive oil

4 cups fresh arugula, cleaned and dried

2 cups fresh spinach, cleaned and dried

¾ cup Sesame Poppy Dressing (recipe follows)

2 ripe pears, sliced vertically and very thin

½ cup Asiago cheese shavings

½ cup shelled walnuts

2 slicing tomatoes, cut ¼-inch thick in half-moon slices
   (use plum tomatoes if slicing tomatoes are not of high quality)

Season the beaten eggs with salt, pepper, garlic, and half the parsley. In another mixing bowl, combine the breadcrumbs with half the Parmesan cheese. Dip the chicken pieces first in the egg mixture, then the breadcrumbs. Be sure they're coated evenly.

Heat the olive oil in a large skillet. Sauté the dredged chicken strips in the hot oil for about 1 minute on each side, until each piece turns opaque and golden brown. Set the chicken aside on paper towels to absorb excess oil.

Toss the arugula and spinach in a large mixing bowl with 3 to 4 tablespoons of the dressing. Add additional dressing if desired, and toss again. Put the tossed greens on a serving platter or individual salad plates, top with pear slices, chicken pieces, cheese shavings, and walnuts. Ring the outer edges of the salad plates with tomato slices, sprinkle with remaining parsley, and serve.

SESAME POPPY DRESSING

Makes I cup

1 cup apple cider vinegar

⅓ cup sugar

¼ cup sesame seeds

¼ cup poppy seeds

¼ cup scallions, chopped, green part only

2 tablespoons Worcestershire sauce

2 tablespoons vegetable oil

Combine all ingredients in the workbowl of a food processor, process for about 15 seconds, and refrigerate for at least 30 minutes to thicken the dressing before serving. Use as directed above.

NOTE: As an alternative, you can use brown sugar or a non-sugar sweetener, making sure to start with no more than 2 packets, then adding a little more if desired.

3

MEAT LOVERS' sauté

⊠

EVEN IN THIS health-conscious "I don't eat meat" society, there are still plenty of people who do. Few flavors are as delicious as a great cut of meat, cooked to perfection, enhanced by a sauce in which the juices of the meat play an integral part. These recipes take full advantage of the flavors and richness of meat.

SAUSAGE WITH BROCCOLI RABE OVER LINGUINE

S AUSAGE PAIRED WITH broccoli rabe is a classic Italian combination. Each has the intensity of flavor to hold its own with the other. Therefore, all you need is a simple sauce, such as an oil-garlic sauce, to complete the dish. The sauce is wonderful even without the pasta, accompanied by some crusty bread.

makes 4 servings

I pound linguine (or other favorite pasta)

4 links sweet Italian sausage

½ cup extra virgin olive oil

I bunch of fresh broccoli rabe, sliced lengthwise, cut in half, and parboiled (see head-note, page 66)

I medium clove garlic, minced

3 to 4 tablespoons white wine

¼ cup chicken broth

Salt and freshly ground black pepper to taste

Cook the pasta according to package directions in a large pot of boiling, salted water.

While the pasta water comes to a boil, put the sausage in a 4-quart pot, cover the meat with water, boil, and cook for 15 minutes. Transfer the meat to a cutting board and slice it into 1-inch pieces.

While the pasta cooks, put the oil in a large sauté pan over medium-high heat for about 1 minute, until the oil is hot but not smoking. Sauté the sausage in the hot oil until the pieces begin to brown on all sides, about 2 minutes. Sauté the broccoli rabe until softened but still firm, about 2 minutes, then sauté the garlic for about 30 seconds, until it begins to turn golden. Deglaze the pan by adding the wine and cooking for 1 minute more. Add the chicken broth and cook for another minute, until the sauce comes to a boil. Remove from the heat and season with salt and pepper.

To serve, drain the pasta and toss it in a serving bowl with the liquid part of the sauce. Adjust the seasoning and put the sausage and rabe on top of the pasta.

RIGATONI BOLOGNESE
WITH TURKEY AND PORK

D AN, A YOUNG college student who worked for us for several years, kept coming in for his weekly dose of Biscotti food even after he left our employ. Almost always, he ordered this classic rigatoni dish. What makes it so good is the use of turkey and pork for the Bolognese sauce instead of the traditional beef and/or veal. Pork is packed with flavor and the turkey adds balance with its leanness and subtlety. This simple dish is easy to make and is sure to become a favorite.

makes 4 servings

3 to 4 tablespoons extra virgin olive oil (or enough to cover the bottom of the pan)

Pinch of red pepper flakes

1 small shallot, finely chopped

½ medium clove garlic, minced

½ pound ground pork

½ pound ground turkey

3 to 4 tablespoons sherry

4 cups Marinara Sauce (page 224)

¼ cup heavy cream

Salt and freshly ground black pepper to taste

1 pound rigatoni

1 tablespoon Italian (flat-leaf) parsley, stems removed and chopped, for garnish

Put the oil and red pepper flakes in a large sauté pan over medium-high heat for about 1 minute and heat until the oil is hot but not smoking. Sauté the chopped shallot until soft, about 1 minute, then sauté the garlic for a few seconds, or just until the garlic begins to brown.

Add the ground meat, and use a wooden spoon to break it into pieces and brown it on all sides, about 3 to 4 minutes. Be careful not to overstir or the meat chunks will be too small and the meat will not brown properly. Add the sherry and stir. Add the Marinara Sauce, and stir occasionally, until the sauce begins to boil. Finish the sauce by adding the cream. Stir, reduce the heat to low, simmer for 1 to 2 more minutes, and remove from the heat. Season with salt and pepper.

While the sauce is cooking, bring a large pot of salted water to a boil, and cook the pasta according to package directions. Drain the cooked pasta and toss it in a serving bowl with about half the liquid part of the sauce. Transfer the pasta to individual serving plates, top it with the remaining sauce, and sprinkle the parsley over each portion.

MEDALLIONS OF PORK WITH DRIED FRUITS

I INVENTED THIS dish when I wanted to do something new with the pork medallions on my menu. I had offered them in a very traditional way, topped with marinara sauce and melted mozzarella. For this dish, I first sautéed the medallions in a white wine sauce, then added a few capers and olives. I had a bag of dried fruit (pears, apricots, prunes, and peaches) lying around, so I experimented and tossed a few assorted fruits in the sauce as well. What resulted was an unusual but delicious dish in which the flavors of the fruits are distinguishable yet mild enough to complement the flavor of the pork. The white wine sauce brings all the flavors together. It's wonderful served with mashed potatoes.

makes 4 servings

4 to 6 tablespoons extra virgin olive oil (or enough to cover the bottom of the pan
  for each batch)

12 slices center-cut boneless pork loin, pounded with a mallet into 1/4-inch-thick
  medallions, about 2 pounds total

20 to 30 pieces dried fruit (such as plums, prunes, apricots, peaches, pears, etc.)

1/2 medium clove garlic, minced

1/4 cup dry white wine

1/4 cup chicken broth

1 cup White Wine Sauce (page 222) (see note)

2 to 3 tablespoons heavy cream (optional)

Salt and freshly ground black pepper to taste

1 tablespoon Italian (flat-leaf) parsley, stems removed and chopped

4 to 5 fresh radicchio leaves (optional garnish)

Preheat the oven to a warming temperature of 200° to 225°F. This dish is best prepared in two batches. Keep the first batch warm in the preheated oven while you prepare the second.

Heat half the oil in a large sauté pan over high heat for about 30 seconds, until the oil is hot but not smoking. Brown 6 of the pork medallions for about 1 minute on each side. Sauté half the fruit and half the garlic for about 15 seconds, until the garlic starts to turn golden brown. Add half the wine, half the broth, and half the White Wine Sauce, and cook until the sauce begins to boil. Stir in half the cream, reduce the heat to low, and simmer for about 1 minute, until the sauce thickens to the consistency of a creamy gravy.

Transfer the contents of the pan to a warm platter and keep warm in the oven while you repeat the above instructions with the remaining oil, pork, fruit, garlic, wine, broth, White Wine Sauce, cream, salt, and pepper.

When finished, remove the platter from the oven, add the second batch of pork medallions and sauce, and sprinkle the parsley on top. Garnish, if desired, with a few radicchio leaves.

NOTE: Remember, if you do not have any White Wine Sauce already made, you can make it right in the sauté pan after the wine is added. Just add 1 tablespoon of flour to the pan liquid, stir to make a paste, and slowly add ½ cup of chicken broth, stirring to make a smooth sauce.

NOTE: This dish can be made a day or two ahead of serving, then warmed, covered, for 15 to 20 minutes (or until the pork in the center of the platter is warm) in a 350°F oven.

PORK AND EGGPLANT PARMESAN

EGGPLANT PARMESAN IS commonly made by breading and frying some sliced eggplant, then layering it with marinara, Parmesan, and mozzarella before baking it. Pork Parmesan is made similarly. My favorite combination is this: alternating layers of pork and eggplant, separated by the marinara, cheese, and a ricotta-béchamel mixture, which adds a wonderful creaminess to the dish. Another bonus: This dish can be prepared and baked in the same sauté pan.

makes 4 servings

6 tablespoons extra virgin olive oil

1 firm, large eggplant, cut the long way into 4 slices, each slice approximately ¼ inch thick and 6 inches long

¼ cup chicken broth

4 slices (each ¼ inch thick) center-cut pork loin, pounded thinner with a mallet, 12 to 16 ounces total

½ medium clove garlic, minced

2 tablespoons red wine

½ cup Marinara Sauce (page 224)

1 cup Ricotta/Béchamel Sauce (page 84)

Approximately 3 tablespoons Parmesan cheese, grated

8 ounces fresh mozzarella cheese, cut in 8 slices

Salt and freshly ground black pepper to taste

1 tablespoon Italian (flat-leaf) parsley, stems removed and chopped

Preheat oven to 350°F. Use a large sauté pan with an ovenproof handle, all-stainless steel, if possible.

Put ¼ cup of the oil in the pan over high heat for about 60 seconds, or until the oil is hot but not smoking. Cook the eggplant slices in the hot oil for about 1 minute, or until brown. Turn. Add half the chicken broth and cook for 1 minute more, or until the second side of the eggplant is golden brown. Remove from the heat. Place the eggplant on paper towels to absorb excess oil. When it is cool enough to handle, cut each piece in half.

Discard any oil remaining in the pan and wipe the pan with a paper towel. Heat the remaining oil in the pan for about 30 seconds over medium-high heat, or until the oil is hot but not smoking, and brown the pork slices on one side in the hot oil for about 1 minute. Cook the garlic for about 30 seconds, or just until the garlic begins to brown. Add the wine, and turn the pork slices. Add the remaining chicken broth, and brown the pork for another minute on the second side. Turn off the heat, and transfer the pork slices to the paper towels with the eggplant.

Now assemble the cooked ingredients. Discard any oil remaining in the pan, and, off the heat, pour half the Marinara Sauce in the pan and place 4 of the eggplant slices atop the sauce. Put a dollop of the Ricotta/Béchamel Sauce on top of each eggplant slice and sprinkle with 1 tablespoon of Parmesan. Top each piece with 1 slice of the mozzarella, a pinch of salt and pepper, and half the parsley.

Top with the pork, another dollop of the Ricotta/Béchamel, another 1 tablespoon of Parmesan, another slice of mozzarella, additional salt and pepper, and the rest of the parsley. For the last layer, top with the remaining eggplant slices and top each with a bit more Marinara Sauce and a sprinkle of Parmesan.

Put the sauté pan in the oven, and bake for about 10 minutes, or until the cheese begins to melt.

NOTE: All components of this recipe can be made a day or two ahead, refrigerated, and assembled and baked shortly before serving. This dish can easily be doubled or tripled to serve more guests. For these larger quantities, use an oblong dish for the baking.

RICOTTA/BÉCHAMEL SAUCE

makes about 1 ¼ cups

2 tablespoons butter

2 tablespoons unbleached white flour

½ cup whole milk

½ cup whole-milk ricotta cheese

Salt and freshly ground black pepper to taste

1 teaspoon Parmesan cheese (optional)

Put the butter in a small saucepan over medium-low heat. Add the flour and stir with a wire whisk until the mixture has formed a paste. Slowly add the milk, whisking constantly, until all the milk is absorbed and the mixture has become a smooth, thick sauce. Cook for 10 more minutes, or until the taste of raw flour has disappeared. Remove from the heat and refrigerate for at least 30 minutes.

Add the ricotta cheese, salt and pepper, and, if desired, the Parmesan. Refrigerate until needed. Use as directed in previous recipe. The remaining sauce can be used as a filling for lasagna or other baked pastas, as a sauce for other pasta or meat dishes, or in omelets. Use as a substitute for creamy cheeses or in combination with other cheeses.

NOTE: This sauce can be made up to 3 days in advance.

versatility

RUNNING A RESTAURANT means, among many other things, that you must be able to cater to the whims and tastes of many different people. Over the years, as I'm sure you can imagine, I've heard them all. "I'd like the salmon and wild mushroom linguine, but could you leave out the mushrooms?" "I'm allergic to garlic, so can I have the Spaghetti with Garlic and Oil without the garlic?" Remember the 1970 movie *Five Easy Pieces* and the Jack Nicholson character? He couldn't get what he wanted in the diner scene without throwing a fit. Unlike that character, we have learned to be accommodating. Besides being nice guys, sautéing helps us. Almost anything can be added to or eliminated from the sauté pan—and easily. So if you have a finicky family member with odd requests, sauté cooking will let you simply respond, "Yes, dear."

FILET MIGNON WITH HORSERADISH MUSTARD WINE SAUCE

I HAVE HAD a variation of this dish on my catering menu for years. A whole filet would be blackened, then grilled and sliced, and served on a platter at room temperature with a horseradish mayonnaise. This platter was and still is such a hit that I decided to try a sautéed version. This is what I came up with. Serve these filets with garlic mashed potatoes. Not only do the two go well together, but the sauce is wonderful with it, too.

makes 4 servings

¼ cup extra virgin olive oil

4 filet mignon steaks, each about 10 ounces, seasoned with salt and freshly ground
    black pepper to taste

1 shallot, sliced

½ medium clove garlic, minced

¼ cup dry white wine

1 cup White Wine Sauce (page 222) or made in the pan (see page 81)

1 tablespoon spicy mustard, or to taste

¼ cup chicken broth

2 tablespoons heavy cream (optional)

2 tablespoons prepared horseradish, or to taste

Salt and freshly ground black pepper to taste

1 tablespoon Italian (flat-leaf) parsley, stems removed and chopped

4 leaves fresh radicchio or other red leaf, for garnish

Put the oil in a large sauté pan over high heat for about 30 seconds, until the oil is hot but not smoking. Brown the steaks in the hot oil for 2 to 3 minutes per side for medium rare. When the meat has reached the desired doneness, remove it from the sauté pan and cook the shallot and garlic for about 1 minute, until the shallot softens.

Add the wine, White Wine Sauce, mustard, and chicken broth, and cook for 1 or 2 minutes, or until the sauce just begins to boil. Stir in the cream and the horseradish, reduce the heat to low, and simmer for about 1 minute, or until the sauce is the consistency of a cream gravy. Season with the salt and pepper.

To serve, cover the bottom of each serving plate with some sauce, top with a filet, and garnish with parsley and a few radicchio leaves.

87

STEAK WITH PEPPERS AND ONIONS IN A TOMATO WINE SAUCE OVER FETTUCCINE

REMEMBER THAT TRIED and true dish, Pepper Steak? The wonderful flavor of sautéed peppers and onions mixed with the pan juices from the strips of sautéed beef, creating a delicious brown gravy that we soaked up with white rice? Because I loved this dish over rice, I knew it would also be delicious over pasta.

makes 4 servings

1 pound fettuccine

¼ cup extra virgin olive oil (or just enough to cover the bottom of the pan)

Pinch of red pepper flakes

1 pound sirloin steak, cut in ¾-inch strips

2 red bell peppers, cut in ½-inch slices

1 large Vidalia or other sweet onion, cut in medium dice

1 medium clove garlic, minced

¼ cup red wine

2 cups Marinara Sauce (page 224)

¼ cup chicken broth

Salt and freshly ground black pepper to taste

1 tablespoon Italian (flat-leaf) parsley, stems removed and chopped

Cook the pasta according to package directions in a large pot of boiling salted water.

While the pasta cooks, put the olive oil and red pepper flakes in a large sauté pan for about 30 seconds over high heat, until the oil is hot but not smoking. Cook the steak and the peppers for about 1 minute, until all sides are nicely browned. Sauté the onion, cooking for about 2 more minutes, until the onions and peppers begin to

é

soften, then add the garlic, cooking for 30 seconds more, or just until the garlic begins to brown. Add the wine and cook for about 1 minute more, then the Marinara Sauce and chicken broth and cook for 3 to 4 minutes more, or just until the sauce begins to boil. Remove from the heat and season with salt and pepper.

Drain the pasta and transfer it to a large serving bowl. Toss the pasta with the liquid part of the sauce, and place the pasta on individual serving plates. Top with the steak, peppers, and onions. Sprinkle each serving with the parsley.

DUCK IN ORANGE FENNEL SAUCE

T HIS ELEGANT DISH is easy to prepare. Breast of duck is first pan-seared and cooked in the sauté pan so the pan juices can be incorporated with a white wine sauce. A splash of orange-flavored liqueur and fresh orange juice adds wonderful flavor to this creamy textured sauce and makes an unforgettable accompaniment to risotto.

makes 4 servings

3 to 4 tablespoons extra virgin olive oil, or enough to cover the bottom of the pan

4 pieces boneless breast of duck, each 8 to 10 ounces, seasoned with salt and freshly ground black pepper to taste

1/4 cup chicken broth

I fresh fennel bulb, core removed and thinly sliced

I tablespoon fennel seeds

1/2 medium clove garlic, minced

2 tablespoons orange-flavored liqueur

2 tablespoons dry white wine

I cup White Wine Sauce (page 222)

I seedless orange, half squeezed for juice, half cut into thin slices

I tablespoon heavy cream (optional)

I tablespoon Italian (flat-leaf) parsley, stems removed and chopped

Put the olive oil in a large sauté pan for about 1 minute over high heat, until the oil is hot but not smoking. Sear the duck breasts (that is, brown them quickly) in the hot oil for about 1 minute on each side before adding the chicken broth. Cook for an additional 4 to 5 minutes, transfer the duck to a baking dish, and set aside.

Cook the fennel slices and fennel seeds in the sauté pan for 1 to 2 minutes, until the fresh fennel begins to soften. Sauté the garlic for a few moments, until it begins to turn golden, then add the liqueur and wine and cook for 1 minute more. Add the White Wine Sauce, and cook for 1 or 2 minutes more, or until the sauce begins to boil, then the orange juice and the cream. Reduce the heat to low and simmer for about 1 minute, until the sauce is the consistency of creamy gravy. Set the sauce aside.

Place the duck breasts, skin side up, about 6 inches from the broiler element. Cook until the skin is crispy and the breast is medium rare, about 2 minutes. Place the breasts onto a cutting board and cut each breast in thin, diagonal slices.

To serve, cover the bottom of each dinner plate with some sauce. Arrange a portion of duck slices on top of the sauce, and garnish with parsley and orange slices.

FETTUCCINE CARBONARA
WITH ARTICHOKES

I N A CARBONARA sauce, the raw egg in the sauce is cooked by the hot pasta. Then, a sauce of cream, Parmesan cheese, and pancetta is added to the pasta. My version adds artichokes and chicken broth to nicely balance the cream and lighten the overall taste of the dish. Pancetta and Parmesan tend to be salty, so don't add salt to the sauce or the pasta.

makes 4 servings

1 pound fettuccine

2 to 3 tablespoons extra virgin olive oil

4 slices pancetta, each ¼ inch thick, diced

½ medium clove garlic, minced

1 can artichoke hearts, packed in water (see note)

¼ cup chicken broth

1 cup heavy cream

¼ cup freshly grated Parmesan cheese

2 medium eggs, beaten

1 tablespoon Italian (flat-leaf) parsley, stems removed and chopped

Freshly ground black pepper to taste

Cook the pasta according to package directions in a large pot of boiling salted water. While the pasta cooks, put the olive oil in a large sauté pan over medium heat for about 30 seconds and brown the pancetta on all sides in the hot oil for about 1 minute. Sauté the garlic for a few moments until it starts to turn golden, then sauté the artichokes for about 15 seconds. Add the chicken broth, cream, and Parmesan, bring to a boil, lower the heat, and simmer for about 1 minute, or until the sauce reaches a thick, creamy consistency. Set aside.

Drain the fettuccine and transfer it to a serving bowl. Toss with the beaten egg, then with half the liquid part of the sauce. Place servings of pasta on individual serving plates, and top each portion with some of the remaining sauce and the solid ingredients in the sauté pan. Sprinkle with parsley, black pepper, and, if desired, a bit more Parmesan. Serve.

NOTE: Artichokes are usually sold in 14-ounce cans that yield about 8½ ounces after draining.

93

VEAL SCALOPPINE WITH
TOMATOES, CAPERS, AND OLIVES

T HE COMBINATION OF capers, olives, and tomatoes makes a classic sauce from southern Italy that is full of flavor and passion. You can use it with just about anything—pasta, pork, chicken, or fish. Once you try this recipe, I'm sure you will use this sauce with many of your favorite ingredients.

makes 4 servings

Approximately ¾ cup extra virgin olive oil

12 slices (each ¼ inch thick) veal, top, or eye round, lightly pounded and dredged in seasoned flour, 2 to 2½ pounds total

1 medium clove garlic, minced

4 plum tomatoes, diced

¼ cup capers, drained

½ cup pitted kalamata olives

¼ cup dry white wine

¼ cup chicken broth

Salt and freshly ground black pepper to taste

1 tablespoon Italian (flat-leaf) parsley, stems removed and chopped

Put 3 to 4 tablespoons of the oil in a large sauté pan over medium-high heat for about 1 minute, until it is hot but not smoking.

Put half the veal slices in the hot oil and cook until browned, about 2 minutes per side. Remove the veal from the pan, keep warm, heat another 3 to 4 tablespoons of oil until the oil is hot but not smoking, and cook the second batch of veal slices in the same manner. Remove them from the pan and keep them warm with the first slices.

To prepare the sauce, discard any oil remaining in the pan, wipe with a paper towel, and put another 3 to 4 tablespoons of oil in the pan, heating until the oil is hot but not smoking. Sauté the garlic for a few seconds, until it begins to turn golden, then add the tomatoes, capers, and olives, and sauté for 1 minute more. Add the wine and broth, and cook for about 1 minute, or until the sauce begins to boil. Reduce the heat to low and simmer the sauce for 1 minute more. Remove from the heat and simmer with salt and pepper.

To serve, put about half the sauce on a warm serving platter. Top with the veal slices and the remaining sauce, and sprinkle with the parsley.

95

VEAL SCALOPPINE
WITH SHIITAKE MUSHROOMS

T HE SHIITAKE MUSHROOMS sautéed in the pan juices from the strips of veal make a heavenly sauce. Serve it alone, with a fresh salad and some crusty bread, and you'll have an elegant dinner that's also quick and easy to prepare. For a variation, serve it over pasta, risotto, or even mashed potatoes. If you don't like veal, the same recipe and cooking procedure work wonderfully with, pork, chicken, or beef.

makes 4 servings

Approximately ¾ cup extra virgin olive oil

12 slices veal, 2 to 2½ pounds total, sliced or pounded to ¼-inch thickness and
   dredged in seasoned flour

4 dozen shiitake mushrooms, cleaned and stems removed

½ medium clove garlic, minced

½ cup dry white wine

½ cup White Wine Sauce (page 222)

2 tablespoons Marinara Sauce (page 224)

2 tablespoons heavy cream (optional)

Salt and freshly ground black pepper to taste

1 tablespoon Italian (flat-leaf) parsley, stems removed and chopped

Put 3 to 4 tablespoons of the olive oil (enough to cover the bottom of the skillet) in a large sauté pan over medium-high heat for about 30 seconds, or until the oil is hot but not smoking. Brown 6 veal slices for about 2 minutes per side, then remove them from the pan and keep them warm. Repeat with another 3 to 4 tablespoons of oil and the remaining veal slices.

After the veal has been removed, discard any remaining oil, wipe the pan with a paper towel, and heat the remaining oil (again, just enough to cover the bottom of the pan) over medium-high heat until the oil is hot but not smoking. Sauté the mushrooms in the hot oil until they begin to soften. Sauté the garlic for a few seconds until it begins to turn golden, and add the wine, White Wine Sauce, and Marinara Sauce. Heat until the sauce comes to a boil. Stir in the cream, reduce the heat, and simmer for about 1 minute, until the sauce thickens.

To serve, put the veal on a serving platter, top with the mushroom sauce, and sprinkle with the parsley.

SAUTÉED FILET MIGNON
WITH VEGETABLES AND SHERRY

THIS RECIPE IS similar to beef stew, only it's much quicker, so the vegetables retain their crunchiness. And, of course, it's all made in a sauté pan. Use the vegetables that I suggest, or substitute those of your own choosing. Serve it by itself or over risotto, rice, potatoes, or pasta.

makes 4 servings

¼ cup extra virgin olive oil

2 pounds beef tenderloin, cut into ½-inch strips

I medium zucchini, cut in medium dice

I medium red bell pepper, cut in medium dice

I medium green bell pepper, cut in medium dice

I medium carrot, cut in medium dice

I medium onion, cut in medium dice

4 plum tomatoes, cut in medium dice

½ medium clove garlic, minced

¼ cup sherry

½ cup White Wine Sauce (page 222)

¼ cup chicken broth

Salt and freshly ground black pepper to taste

I tablespoon Italian (flat-leaf) parsley, stems removed and chopped

Put the olive oil in a large skillet over medium-high heat for about 30 seconds, until the oil is hot but not smoking, and brown the beef on all sides in the hot oil. Sauté the zucchini, bell peppers, carrot, onion, and tomatoes for about 1 minute, then sauté the garlic for a few seconds, until it begins to turn golden. Add the sherry, White Wine Sauce, and chicken broth, and sauté until all ingredients have softened but are still firm and the sauce has thickened and comes to a boil.

To serve, transfer the contents of the pan to a warm serving platter, season with salt and pepper, and sprinkle with parsley.

4

SAUTÉED seafood

⊠

SEAFOOD HAS SO many characteristics that determine and affect the proper cooking method that it becomes just too complicated for most cooks. Now, I come along wanting you to sauté it! "No way," you say. Yet even shellfish can be cooked in a skillet. The recipes in this chapter will take the fear out of preparing seafood for even the most inexperienced cook. The results, like so many sautéed dishes, are nothing short of heavenly.

First, here are a few things you should know about cleaning and storing seafood:

Clams and Mussels. Most of the recipes in this book call for sautéing the clams and mussels while they are still in their shells. This means that they must be bought live, so buy them as fresh as possible. When selecting live clams or mussels, make sure that the shells are closed tightly, or, if slightly opened, that they close when prodded. If not, don't buy them. Store them on a bed of ice, uncovered. Remember, they are alive and must breathe. It's best to use them within a day or two of purchase to ensure freshness.

Manila Clams and Prince Edward Island mussels, the varieties used in the recipes in this book, are, like most of the clams and mussels available today, farm-raised. This makes cleaning them relatively easy. These varieties are also easy to cook because they are small and open easily when steamed or sautéed.

Clean clams and mussels by scrubbing the shells with a stiff brush under cold running water and discarding any that do not close when prodded. Occasionally, you may come across a mussel with a beard, the hairlike fiber that the mussel uses to attach itself to rocks. Remove this beard by simply pulling or cutting it out.

Calamari. Calamari, or squid, are rather difficult and time-consuming to clean, especially the tentacles, so I suggest buying tubes, which have already been cleaned. Buy them fresh or frozen and store them covered in the refrigerator, on a bed of ice. (Drain and replace with a bed of fresh ice in the morning.) Calamari should be cooked quickly, over high heat, for 2 to 3 minutes (perfect for sautéing) or boiled for an hour. Either method will prevent the calamari from getting rubbery.

Shrimp. There are thousands of varieties of shrimp in the world, and they come in many sizes. Choose whichever ones you prefer as long as they are fresh and used within 24 hours of purchase or are kept frozen until the day you plan to use them. If fresh, store them in a recloseable freezer bag on a bed of ice until ready to cook. Shrimp, cleaned and deveined, can readily be purchased in most supermarkets. If not, cleaning and prepping shrimp are very easy: Remove the head, pull off the legs on the inside curve, and peel off the outer shell. Devein by slicing, with a small knife, along the outer curve of the shrimp and pulling off the dark vein. Then rinse the shrimp under cold running water.

Fish Fillets. Store in a recloseable freezer bag on a bed of ice in the refrigerator.

SALMON AND WILD MUSHROOMS IN A ROASTED RED PEPPER SAUCE OVER FETTUCCINE

I F YOU LIKE mushrooms and salmon, this dish will astound you. The roasted red pepper sauce is easy to prepare, even though it is somewhat time-consuming to roast and peel the red bell peppers. You can buy roasted peppers in the supermarket, but I assure you that once you learn how to roast your own, you'll never go back to store-bought ones. You'll love serving roasted peppers tossed with a bit of oil, garlic, salt, pepper, and parsley or basil as an accompaniment to many meals.

makes 4 servings

Approximately ½ cup extra virgin olive oil

½ pound wild mushrooms (shiitake, cremino, portabello, or other favorite), stems removed, cleaned, and sliced

2 medium cloves garlic, minced

1 pound fettuccine (or other favorite pasta, except small, shaped pasta)

Red pepper flakes to taste

1 pound salmon fillet, skinned and cut into 1-inch pieces

2 tablespoons sherry

1 cup Marinara Sauce (page 224)

3 large red bell peppers, roasted and puréed

¼ cup dry-packed sun-dried tomatoes, sliced

½ cup fish broth

2 tablespoons heavy cream (optional)

Salt and freshly ground black pepper to taste

1 tablespoon Italian (flat-leaf) parsley, stems removed and chopped

Heat about half the olive oil, enough to cover the pan, in a large skillet over high heat for about 30 seconds, until the oil is hot but not smoking. Add the mushroom slices and half the garlic and cook until the mushrooms are soft but still firm, about 3 to 4 minutes. Set aside. Remove the mushrooms from the pan into the plate.

Cook the pasta according to package directions in a large pot of boiling, salted water.

While the pasta cooks, put the remaining olive oil and the red pepper flakes in the same skillet over high heat for about 30 seconds, or until the oil is hot but not smoking. Brown the salmon in the hot oil for about 1 minute on all sides, add the remaining garlic, and cook briefly, until the garlic begins to turn golden brown. Add the sherry, return the mushrooms to the pan, cook for 1 minute, and add the Marinara Sauce, puréed peppers, sun-dried tomato slices, and fish broth. Cook for 1 to 2 minutes, or until the sauce starts to boil. Reduce the heat to low, stir in the cream, and simmer for 1 minute more, until the sauce thickens. Add a bit more broth if the sauce is too thick, and season with salt and pepper.

To serve, drain the pasta and toss it in a large serving bowl with the liquid portion of the sauce. Transfer the pasta to individual serving plates and top each serving with the sautéed ingredients. Adjust seasoning, and sprinkle with parsley.

roasting peppers

THE BEST ROASTED pepper of all is the one you roast yourself, in your own kitchen. It's not hard. Place as many bell peppers as you wish on a foil-lined baking sheet a few inches from the broiler element of your oven. When the exposed sides are blackened, turn the peppers with a pair of tongs. When the entire pepper has blackened, remove them from the oven and place them in a brown paper bag. When they're cool enough to handle, rub the blackened skins. The skins will magically slip off, and you'll be left with a roasted pepper that can then be sliced and used in other recipes. One warning: Don't wash the blackened skins off, or the flavorful oils will wash away as well.

CALAMARI IN WHITE WINE SAUCE OVER LINGUINE

T HIS RECIPE IS a variation of the calamari on page 36. The oil, garlic, wine, and tomatoes make a sauce so delicious that it's just wonderful over pasta. This dish can be ready to serve in minutes.

makes 4 servings

1 pound linguine

¼ cup extra virgin olive oil

Pinch of red pepper flakes

1 pound calamari tubes, cut into ½-inch pieces

½ medium clove garlic, minced

2 scallions, sliced, white and green parts

1 plum tomato, diced

3 to 4 tablespoons dry white wine

3 to 4 tablespoons White Wine Sauce (page 222)

¼ cup fish broth or clam juice

2 tablespoons pine nuts

1 tablespoon Italian (flat-leaf) parsley, stems removed and chopped

Salt and freshly ground black pepper to taste

Cook the pasta according to package directions in a large pot of boiling, salted water. While the pasta cooks, put the oil and the red pepper flakes in a large skillet over high heat for about 30 seconds, until the oil is hot but not smoking. Cook the calamari tubes for about 1 minute, then sauté the garlic, scallions, and tomato for 30 seconds more, or just until the garlic begins to brown. Add the wine, White Wine Sauce, and fish broth and cook for 1 minute more, or until the sauce begins to boil. Remove the pan from the heat and add the pine nuts and parsley.

To serve, drain the pasta and toss it with half the liquid portion of the sauce in a large serving bowl. Transfer the pasta to individual serving plates, and top each serving with the remaining liquid sauce and the solid part of the sauce, season with salt and pepper, and serve immediately

NOTE: Depending on the thickness of the calamari, it may need another minute or so of cooking. Taste a piece. It should be opaque and tender. If not, keep it on the heat for another minute. If the sauce has become too thick, add a bit more fish broth before removing the pan from the heat.

toss and turn

I LOVE TOSSING the ingredients in my sauté pan by flipping my wrist and watching the contents sail in the air and return to the sauté pan. You've all seen chefs do this on television, but it takes practice. It certainly has no effect on the outcome of the dish you're preparing. A fork or a pair of tongs, which I highly recommend—they're so useful for turning, stirring, grabbing, tossing—will work just fine.

SEAFOOD RISOTTO

S EAFOOD RISOTTO IS usually made with the seafood cooked right into the risotto, as you stir. Although it makes a wonderful dish, I find that the seafood can easily become overcooked and get lost in the risotto, or that some diners can get lots while others get cheated. I find that flavoring the risotto with a seafood broth and then topping it with sautéed seafood is an unbeatable combination.

makes 4 to 6 servings

1 pound risotto, made from Arborio rice prepared according to package directions and kept warm (see note)

¼ cup extra virgin olive oil

Red pepper flakes to taste

2 dozen small clams, rinsed

2 dozen small mussels, cleaned and debearded

12 large sea scallops

12 medium to large shrimp, shelled, cleaned, and deveined

½ medium clove garlic, minced

3 plum tomatoes, diced

2 to 3 tablespoons dry white wine

¼ cup White Wine Sauce (page 222)

¼ cup clam juice or fish broth

2 tablespoons heavy cream (optional)

1 tablespoon butter (optional)

Salt and freshly ground black pepper to taste

1 tablespoon Italian (flat-leaf) parsley, stems removed and chopped

4 to 6 lemon wedges, for garnish

Prepare the risotto. Either keep the finished risotto warm in a 200°F oven or cook it while you prepare the rest of this recipe.

Put the olive oil and red pepper flakes in a large sauté pan over high heat for about 30 seconds, or until the oil is hot but not smoking. Cook the clams, mussels, and scallops (on both sides) for 3 to 5 minutes, or until the clams begin to open and the scallops begin to turn opaque. Add the shrimp and cook everything for 1 minute more, until the shrimp turn pink on one side. Turn the shrimp, add the garlic, and cook for a few seconds, until the garlic begins to turn golden.

Cook the tomatoes for another 30 seconds. Add the wine, White Wine Sauce, and clam juice or fish broth, and cook for about 1 minute more, just until the sauce begins to boil. Reduce the heat to low, add the butter and cream if desired, simmer for about a minute until the sauce thickens, remove from the heat, and season with salt and pepper.

To serve, stir some of the liquid part of the sauce into the risotto, then spoon the risotto onto individual serving plates. Top each serving with the remainder of the sauce and the seafood. If desired, arrange the mussels all along the rim of the platter or plate, then add the seafood in the center. Sprinkle with the parsley, salt and pepper, and garnish each serving plate with a lemon wedge.

NOTE: Arborio rice, for making risotto, is sold in 1-kilogram boxes (2.2 pounds) and comes in two packages. The cooking time is about 15 minutes, but it's best prepared slightly underdone because it will continue cooking after it's removed from the heat.

SHRIMP IN PUTTANESCA SAUCE OVER LINGUINE

P UTTANESCA SAUCE (SEE HEADNOTE, page 178) with its capers, olives, toma-toes, and anchovy, is a wonderful sauce for seafood. You can make this dish with shrimp, as I do in this recipe, or use your own favorite seafood—scallops, cala-mari, clams, mussels, or all.

makes 4 servings

1 pound linguine

2 to 3 tablespoons extra virgin olive oil

Pinch of red pepper flakes

2 anchovy fillets, chopped

2 dozen medium or large shrimp, cleaned and deveined

½ medium clove garlic, minced

1 to 2 tablespoons dry red wine

2 cups Marinara Sauce (page 224)

2 to 3 tablespoon fish broth

2 tablespoons kalamata olives, pitted

1 tablespoon capers, drained

Salt and freshly ground black pepper to taste

1 tablespoon Italian (flat-leaf) parsley, stems removed and chopped

Cook the pasta according to package directions in a large pot of boiling, salted water.

A few minutes before the pasta will be finished, put the olive oil, red pepper flakes, and anchovies in a large sauté pan over high heat for about 30 seconds, or until the oil is hot but not smoking.

Cook the shrimp briefly on one side, just until they begin to turn pink, and turn them. Sauté the garlic for a few seconds, until it begins to turn golden, then add the wine and cook for a few seconds more. Add the Marinara Sauce, fish broth, olives, and capers and cook for about 1 minute more, or until the shrimp are done and the sauce begins to boil. Remove from the heat.

To serve, drain the pasta and toss it in a large serving bowl with half the liquid portion of the sauce. Put the pasta on individual serving plates, and top each with the remaining sauce and the shrimp. Sprinkle with parsley.

111

SPAGHETTI RUSTICA WITH CLAMS IN AN INTENSELY FLAVORED SAUCE

I INVENTED THE sauce for this dish by mixing ordinary tomato sauce with a bit of fish broth and my White Wine Sauce. Though simple, almost rustic, this sauce is inventive and delicious. I guarantee you'll love this dish, even if you don't like anchovies. For anchovy lovers who can't wait to try this recipe, don't tell your family or your guests what's in it until after they've tried it. Anchovies just scare too many people away from trying something delicious.

makes 4 servings

1 pound spaghetti

¼ cup extra virgin olive oil

Pinch of red pepper flakes

3 to 4 shallots, chopped

2 dozen small clams

½ medium clove garlic, minced

4 anchovy fillets, chopped

2 tablespoons dry white wine

1 cup Marinara Sauce (page 224)

½ cup White Wine Sauce (page 222)

¼ cup fish broth

3 tablespoons heavy cream

Salt and freshly ground black pepper to taste

1 tablespoon Italian (flat-leaf) parsley, stems removed and chopped

¼ cup breadcrumbs, lightly toasted (see note)

Cook the pasta according to package directions in a large pot of boiling, salted water.

A few minutes before the pasta will be finished cooking, put the olive oil and red pepper flakes in a large sauté pan over high heat for about 30 seconds, until the oil is hot but not smoking.

Cook the shallots for about 1 minute, or until they soften. Add the clams and cook for 2 to 3 minutes, or until they begin to open, then sauté the garlic briefly, until it begins to turn golden brown. Cook the anchovies and wine for about 30 seconds, then the Marinara Sauce, White Wine Sauce, and fish broth for about 2 more minutes, or until the sauce begins to boil. Reduce the heat, add the cream, stir, and simmer for another minute. Remove from the heat and season with salt and pepper.

To serve, drain the pasta and toss it in a large bowl with about half the liquid portion of the sauce. Divide the pasta among individual serving plates, top each serving with additional sauce and the clams, and sprinkle with parsley and breadcrumbs.

NOTE: To toast the breadcrumbs, spread them on a sheet in the toaster oven, and broil until done (about 1 minute or less).

SCALLOPS IN PESTO-WINE SAUCE OVER FETTUCCINE

I FIND PESTO sauce a bit too intense by itself. But mixing it with a basic white wine sauce tones it down just enough for me, while leaving it rich enough to stand up to large sea scallops. A pesto sauce alone might overwhelm the scallops' flavor. The red peppers provide just the right contrasting flavor and color.

makes 4 servings

½ cup Pesto Sauce (store-bought, or use recipe that follows)

1 pound fettuccine (or other favorite pasta)

3 to 4 tablespoons extra virgin olive oil

16 to 20 sea scallops

1 red bell pepper, cut in strips

½ medium clove garlic, minced

3 to 4 tablespoons white wine

¼ cup fish broth

1 cup White Wine Sauce (page 222)

1 tablespoon heavy cream (optional)

Salt and freshly ground black pepper to taste

If you're preparing pesto sauce for this recipe, do that while you bring the pasta water to a boil. Cook the pasta according to package directions in a large pot of boiling, salted water.

While the pasta cooks, put the olive oil in a large skillet over high heat for about 30 seconds, until the oil is hot but not smoking. Cook the scallops for about 1 minute, until they are brown on one side, turn, and cook on the second side for 1 minute more with the pepper strips. Add the garlic, wine, and fish broth, and cook for 2 to 3 more minutes, until the scallops begin to turn opaque and the peppers have begun to soften. Stir in the White Wine Sauce and the Pesto Sauce and cook for another minute, or until the sauce begins to boil. Stir in the cream, reduce the heat to low, and simmer for about 1 minute, until the sauce has thickened. Remove from the heat and season with salt and pepper. Add a bit more fish broth if the sauce is too thick.

To serve, drain the pasta and toss it in a serving bowl with about half the liquid portion of the sauce. Put the pasta on individual serving plates and top each serving with additional sauce and the scallops.

PESTO SAUCE

I LOVE MAKING pesto sauce using basil and parsley, as this recipe does, instead of just basil. Because the parsley mellows the flavor, the sauce is not as intense when made this way.

makes about 1 cup

1 cup fresh basil leaves, loosely packed

1 cup Italian (flat-leaf) parsley, stems removed and loosely packed

½ cup extra virgin olive oil

¼ cup pine nuts

2 medium cloves garlic

⅓ cup freshly grated Parmesan or Romano cheese

Salt to taste

Put the basil, parsley, oil, pine nuts, and garlic in the workbowl of a food processor, and process until smooth. Pour the sauce into a bowl and stir in the grated cheese. Add salt. Use as directed in previous recipe.

TUNA WITH OLIVES AND TOMATOES

O LIVES AND TOMATOES are a perfect pairing. This sauce works wonderfully with tuna because it is quick and flavorful, so the tuna, which should be cooked medium-rare, will not get overcooked even if it's prepared in the same pan with the sauce. This dish can be served alone, with risotto, or with pasta.

makes 4 servings

3 to 4 tablespoons extra virgin olive oil

Red pepper flakes to taste

2 pounds fresh tuna (yellowfin is best), cut into 1-inch strips

1/2 medium clove garlic, minced

2 anchovy fillets, chopped

4 plum tomatoes, diced

1/4 cup dry white wine

1 cup kalamata olives, pitted

1/4 cup fish broth

Salt and freshly ground black pepper to taste

3 to 4 fresh basil leaves, sliced (for garnish)

Put the olive oil and red pepper flakes in a large sauté pan over medium-high heat for about 30 seconds, until the oil is hot but not smoking. Cook the tuna in the hot oil for about 1 minute per side. (If you prefer your tuna rare, remove it from the pan at this point.)

Sauté the garlic and anchovy for a few seconds, until the garlic begins to turn golden brown, then cook the tomatoes for about 30 seconds, until the tomato begins to soften. Add the wine, cook briefly, then cook the olives and fish broth for another minute, or until the sauce begins to boil. Remove from the heat and season with salt and pepper.

To serve, put the sauce, without the tuna, on a warm serving platter or on individual plates. Top with the tuna, garnish with the basil, and serve immediately.

SHERRIED SHRIMP WITH ROASTED RED PEPPERS OVER LINGUINE

S O MUCH OF cooking involves putting the right ingredients together to create magic. Obviously, some combinations work better than others. This recipe works because the ingredients all blend together to give you lots of flavor in every bite. This is sauté magic.

makes 4 servings

1 pound linguine

3 to 4 tablespoons extra virgin olive oil

Red pepper flakes to taste

2 dozen medium or large shrimp, shelled, cleaned, and deveined

½ medium clove garlic, minced

¼ cup sherry

1 cup Marinara Sauce (page 224)

½ cup roasted red peppers, cut into ¼-inch strips

2 to 3 tablespoons heavy cream

Salt and freshly ground black pepper to taste

1 tablespoon Italian (flat-leaf) parsley, stems removed and chopped

A few minutes before you prepare the sauce, cook the pasta according to package directions in a large pot of boiling, salted water.

While the pasta cooks, put the olive oil and red pepper flakes in a large skillet over medium-high heat for about 30 seconds, or until the oil is hot but not smoking. Sauté the shrimp for less than a minute, until they begin to turn pink, flip them, and add the garlic to the pan. Cook briefly, until the garlic begins to turn golden brown, then add the sherry and cook for about 30 seconds. Add the Marinara Sauce and pepper

⊠

**BRUSCHETTA WITH TOMATOES, FRESH MOZZARELLA,
BASIL, AND KALAMATA OLIVES** (page 30)

CHICKEN-PEAR-ARUGULA SALAD WITH SESAME POPPY DRESSING (page 72)

PIZZA WITH TOMATO-PESTO AND GOAT CHEESE (page 174)

⊠

LINGUINE WITH CHICKEN, ASPARAGUS, BACON, AND SUN-DRIED TOMATOES (page 56)

SEAFOOD RISOTTO (page 108)

⊠

**SALMON AND WILD MUSHROOMS IN A ROASTED RED PEPPER SAUCE
OVER FETTUCCINE** (page 104)

ROASTED VEGETABLES OVER PENNE (page 160)

**LEMON CHICKEN WITH ARTICHOKE HEARTS AND
RED PEPPERS IN A WHITE WINE SAUCE** (page 62)

strips to the pan and cook for 1 minute, or until the sauce comes to a boil. Reduce the heat to low, add the cream, simmer for about 1 minute more, and remove the pan from the heat. Season with salt and pepper.

To serve, drain the pasta and toss it in a large serving bowl with half the liquid portion of the sauce. Divide the pasta among individual serving plates, top with the remaining sauce and the shrimp, sprinkle with the parsley, and serve immediately.

119

SEAFOOD IN A BRANDY WINE SAUCE OVER LINGUINE

T HIS RECIPE WAS a relatively late addition to Biscotti's dinner menu. I added it in the summer of 2001, intending to keep it only for the summer menu. From the moment it appeared, it has been a best seller, so it has remained on the menu ever since. The brandy and spices in the sauce give a subtle bite to a combination of some of the most popular seafood. Serve this dish over linguine, as in the recipe below, over risotto, or even alone. It looks and tastes rich, but, as you can see, it has very little cream and butter, all of which can be eliminated if you really want to cut back on fat.

makes 4 servings

1 pound linguine

4 to 5 tablespoons extra virgin olive oil

Pinch of red pepper flakes

1 dozen sea scallops

1 dozen medium or large shrimp, peeled, cleaned, and deveined

1 pound lobster meat (see note)

½ medium clove garlic, minced

3 to 4 tablespoons brandy

1 cup White Wine Sauce (page 222)

¼ cup fish broth

2 to 3 tablespoons heavy cream (optional)

Old Bay seasoning (see note)

Freshly ground black pepper to taste

1 tablespoon Italian (flat-leaf) parsley, stems removed and chopped

Cook the pasta according to package directions in a large pot of boiling, salted water.

While the pasta cooks, put the olive oil and red pepper flakes in a large skillet over medium-high heat for about 30 seconds. Cook the scallops in the hot oil for about 1 to 2 minutes on each side, until they begin to turn golden brown. Cook the shrimp for about 1 minute, or until they just begin to turn pink on each side. (Remember, shrimp can overcook easily, so don't wait until the shrimp are fully cooked; when they are opaque in the center, proceed.) Sauté the lobster and garlic, cooking just until the garlic begins to turn golden brown.

Add the brandy and cook for about 30 seconds more. Add the White Wine Sauce and fish broth and cook for another minute or so, until the sauce begins to boil. Add the cream, lower the heat, and simmer for 1 minute, until the sauce thickens and the scallops are opaque in the center. Season with Old Bay and pepper. Remove from the heat.

To serve, drain the pasta and toss it in a serving bowl with about half the liquid portion of the sauce. Divide the pasta among individual serving plates and top it with the remaining sauce and the seafood. Sprinkle with the parsley and serve.

NOTE: Lobster meat comes from the tail, knuckle, and claw. It can be purchased fresh from your seafood vendor (although this can be quite expensive) or bought frozen in 2-pound vacuum-packed packages. I use the frozen all the time and it is delicious.

NOTE: Old Bay Seasoning is a wonderful combination of herbs and spices that is perfect for seafood. Use it sparingly because it is salty. (You can always add more.) It is readily available in supermarkets and seafood stores.

5

VEGETARIAN saut√©

⊠

WHENEVER I ASK my students whether they sauté at home, the usual answer is yes, they sauté vegetables. I suppose this is the Sauté Comfort Zone for most people. The goal of this book is to expand that zone, and the recipes in this book are testimony that far more than vegetables can be sautéed. But that's no reason to ignore vegetables. Far from it. Few dishes are more delicious than sautéed vegetables. When you incorporate the vegetables into a sauce for pasta or risotto, it's even better.

tossing pasta

THIS TRICK WILL change your life. Tossing pasta comes as naturally to me as breathing, but so many people toss their pasta only to watch all the good stuff fall to the bottom that I can't keep this to myself any longer. Don't just transfer the entire sauce from pan to pasta bowl. Instead, toss the pasta only with half of the liquid. The flavorful liquid will be easy to toss with a pound of pasta in a large bowl, and the result will be pasta that's nicely coated with liquid. Transfer that pasta to individual serving plates (usually four of them). Then spoon some of the sauce liquid remaining in the pan over the pasta on each serving plate, then spoon the solids (seafood, chicken, meat, vegetables, whatever) over each serving. That's it. Sprinkle the plates with herbs, garnish if you wish, and serve. Everyone has a fair share of the good stuff.

WILD MUSHROOMS WITH GORGONZOLA OVER FETTUCCINE

I F ITALIANS USED cremino, shiitake, and portabello mushrooms in their cooking, this dish would be classic Italian. But they don't. When I was in Italy in 1998, I could not find these mushrooms on any menus. Although this dish sounds very Italian, it's anything but. It's just another example of how I use contemporary ingredients and cook the way Italians would cook if they had the same tastes and ingredients on hand as Americans have. It's also another way I use sauté. This recipe features a cream sauce that's distinctly lighter than most others. That's because I combine it with the White Wine Sauce and infuse it with the juices of the wild mushrooms. So enjoy this dish without feeling bloated.

makes 4 servings

1 pound fettuccine

3 to 4 tablespoons extra virgin olive oil

Pinch of red pepper flakes

1 cup each shiitake, portabello, cremino mushrooms, or any combination

½ medium clove garlic, minced

¼ cup dry white wine

¼ cup dry-packed sun-dried tomatoes, slivered

1 cup White Wine Sauce (page 222)

1 cup heavy cream

¼ cup chicken broth

¼ cup Gorgonzola cheese, crumbled

Salt and freshly ground black pepper to taste

1 tablespoon Italian (flat-leaf) parsley, stems removed and chopped

Cook the pasta according to package directions in a large pot of boiling, salted water.

While the pasta cooks, put the olive oil and red pepper flakes in a large skillet over medium-high heat for about 30 seconds. Cook the mushrooms for 2 to 3 minutes, or just until they begin to soften, then sauté the garlic briefly, until it starts to turn golden. Add the wine, sun-dried tomatoes, White Wine Sauce, cream, and chicken broth, and cook for 2 to 3 minutes, or until the sauce begins to thicken and comes to a boil. Sprinkle in the Gorgonzola, stir to incorporate, and remove from the heat. Season with salt and pepper. Remove the pan from the heat.

To serve, drain the pasta and toss it in a large bowl with about half the liquid portion of the sauce. Divide the pasta among individual serving plates, top with a bit more liquid sauce and the mushrooms, and sprinkle with the parsley.

TOMATOES WITH GOAT CHEESE AND ARUGULA OVER ANGEL HAIR PASTA

THIS DISH IS a personal favorite. It's a perfect blend of simple ingredients that, when combined, is brilliant. I think of this dish as a wonderful culinary example of that old wise saying, "The whole is greater than the sum of its parts."

makes 4 servings

1 pound angel hair pasta

3 to 4 tablespoons extra virgin olive oil

Pinch of red pepper flakes

½ medium clove garlic, minced

12 plum tomatoes, cut in medium dice

3 to 4 tablespoons dry white wine

½ cup Marinara Sauce (page 224)

½ cup chicken broth

Salt and freshly ground black pepper to taste

¼ cup goat cheese, crumbled

7 or 8 fresh arugula leaves, slivered

Cook the pasta according to package directions in a large pot of boiling, salted water.

While the pasta cooks, put the olive oil, red pepper flakes, and garlic in a large skillet over medium-high heat for about 30 seconds, or just until the garlic begins to brown. Cook the tomatoes for about 30 seconds, or until they just begin to soften, then add the wine and cook for 1 minute more. Add the Marinara Sauce and chicken broth, bring to a boil, reduce heat, and simmer for about 1 minute, or until the sauce is a light broth and the tomatoes are softened yet still firm. Remove from the heat and season with salt and pepper.

To serve, drain the pasta and toss it in a large bowl with about half the liquid portion of the sauce. Divide the pasta among individual serving plates, top each serving with some of the remaining liquid, and distribute the tomatoes among the servings. Top each serving with goat cheese and sprinkle with the slivered arugula.

FETTUCCINE IN A FENNEL AND RED BELL PEPPER SAUCE

T IRED OF THE same old vegetables? Try fresh fennel. Its wonderful licorice flavor enhances many a recipe. Fennel, known as *finocchio* in Italian, sort of looks like celery, but that's the end of the similarity. Fennel has a distinct anise flavor and can be eaten raw, served with cheese and fruit as the Italians do, or cooked. This versatile vegetable can be grilled, roasted, baked, or sautéed.

makes 4 servings

1 pound fettuccine

4 to 5 tablespoons extra virgin olive oil

Pinch of red pepper flakes

1 fresh fennel bulb, core removed and thinly sliced

1 teaspoon fennel seeds, crushed

1 red bell pepper, core and seeds removed, thinly sliced

1 medium clove garlic, minced

1 plum tomato, cut in medium dice

3 to 4 tablespoons white wine

¼ cup White Wine Sauce (page 222)

¼ cup chicken broth

1 tablespoon heavy cream (optional)

Salt and freshly ground black pepper to taste

1 tablespoon Italian (flat-leaf) parsley, stems removed and chopped

Cook the pasta according to package directions in a large pot of boiling, salted water. While the pasta cooks, heat the olive oil and red pepper flakes in a large skillet over medium-high heat for about 30 seconds, until the oil is hot but not smoking. Sauté the fennel, fennel seeds, and pepper slices for about 2 minutes, or until the vegetables begin to soften.

Sauté the garlic briefly, until it turns golden brown, and add the tomato, cooking for 1 minute more. Add the wine and cook for 1 more minute, then the White Wine Sauce and chicken broth and cook for 1 more minute, or just until the sauce begins to boil. Reduce the heat, add the cream, and simmer until the sauce is the consistency of heavy cream. Season with salt and pepper. If the sauce is too thick, add a bit more chicken broth.

To serve, drain the pasta and toss in a bowl with half the liquid portion of the sauce. Divide the pasta among individual serving plates and top each serving with a bit more sauce and the vegetables. Sprinkle with the parsley.

SAUTÉED MIXED VEGETABLES
IN A CREAMY ALFREDO WINE SAUCE
OVER FETTUCCINE

H ERE WE HAVE the standard mixed vegetables, but they're served in anything but the standard way. I love to mix a classic alfredo sauce with my White Wine Sauce. It offers a way of satisfying our craving for a rich, creamy sauce without causing us to feel stuffed after three bites. In combination with all the juices and flavors from your favorite vegetables, it's almost decadent. You will also love serving this sauce over mashed potatoes, polenta, or risotto.

makes 4 servings

1 pound fettuccine

3 to 4 tablespoons extra virgin olive oil

Pinch of red pepper flakes

4 cups vegetables (such as carrot, red bell pepper, broccoli, onion, zucchini, eggplant, or other favorites), peeled, cleaned, and cut in medium dice

½ medium clove garlic, minced

3 to 4 tablespoons dry white wine

½ cup White Wine Sauce (page 222)

½ cup heavy cream

1 tablespoon freshly grated Parmesan cheese, or more

2 tablespoons chicken broth

Salt and freshly ground black pepper to taste

1 tablespoon Italian (flat-leaf) parsley, stems removed and chopped

Cook the pasta according to package directions in a large pot of boiling, salted water.

While the pasta cooks, heat the olive oil and red pepper flakes in a large skillet over medium-high heat for about 30 seconds, until the oil is hot but not smoking. Cook the hard vegetables (such as the carrots, broccoli, peppers, and eggplant) for about 2 minutes, then add the softer vegetables (such as the onions and zucchini) and cook for 2 minutes more, or until all the vegetables begin to soften. Sauté the garlic briefly, until it begins to turn golden brown, then add the wine and cook for about 1 minute.

Add the White Wine Sauce, cream, and the 1 tablespoon of Parmesan. Bring to a boil and let the sauce reduce for 1 or 2 minutes. Add the chicken broth, bring to a boil, reduce the heat, and simmer for 1 minute more. Remove from the heat and season with salt and pepper.

To serve, drain the pasta and toss in a bowl with half the liquid portion of the sauce. Divide the pasta among individual serving plates, top each serving with a bit more sauce, the vegetables, and additional Parmesan cheese, if desired. Sprinkle with parsley.

133

BROCCOLI RABE IN AN OIL-GARLIC-TOMATO SAUCE OVER LINGUINE

BROCCOLI RABE IS a strong-flavored vegetable, so the simpler the sauce, the better. That's why cooking it *à la alio e olio* (with garlic and oil) is a classic dish throughout Italy. With the exception of adding tomato to the sauce, my version changes this simple method very little. I love the contrast that fresh tomato adds to this sauce as well as how this addition adds liquid and color. As I've said elsewhere in this book, one of my pet peeves is making a pasta sauce and then not having enough sauce to toss the pasta. In this case, you would have to add more oil in order to yield more sauce. I found that by adding the tomatoes and a bit of chicken broth, I didn't need to do that. Just be careful not to add too much broth or it will change the flavor of this wonderful sauce.

makes 4 servings

1 pound linguine

1 bunch (about 1 pound) broccoli rabe

¾ cup extra virgin olive oil

Pinch of red pepper flakes

1 large clove garlic, minced

2 plum tomatoes, cut in medium dice

¼ cup chicken broth

Salt and freshly ground black pepper to taste

1 tablespoon Italian (flat-leaf) parsley, stems removed and chopped

Cook the pasta according to package directions in a large pot of boiling, salted water. Cut off the thick stalks at the end of the broccoli rabe (a couple of inches or so, depending on the stalk), and, if any of the stalks are thick, slice them in half the long way. Rinse thoroughly, then parboil for a minute or two, until the stalks have softened but are still firm. Drain.

While the pasta cooks, put the olive oil and red pepper flakes in a large skillet over medium-high heat for about 60 seconds, until the oil is hot but not smoking. Cook the broccoli rabe in the hot oil for about 2 minutes. Sauté the garlic briefly, just until it begins to turn golden brown, then cook the tomatoes for 1 more minute. Add the chicken broth and cook until the sauce comes to a boil. Remove from the heat and season with salt and pepper.

To serve, drain the pasta and toss it in a bowl with half the liquid portion of the sauce. Divide the pasta among individual serving plates and top each portion with a bit more sauce and the broccoli rabe. Sprinkle with parsley.

6

LOW-FAT sauté

I'VE SERVED A low-fat sauté menu at my restaurant for many years and its popularity continues to astound me. Like so many other food people, I didn't quite believe that anything low in fat could taste good until I started experimenting with various combinations of ingredients and ways of adding flavor without the fat. I discovered that it could be done quite easily.

The combinations for sautéed low-fat dishes are almost endless. The major change is that you are substituting a broth—chicken, fish, or vegetable, for example—for the olive oil. The raw ingredients cook in the broth and, as the broth evaporates to almost nothing, soak up its flavor and begin to brown. That's when you add the sauce and the rest of the ingredients. This process makes for a very flavorful sauce, even though you haven't used olive oil.

The recipes in this chapter are some of the results of my efforts. They reveal simple secrets and steps to romance the palate and create delicious, low-fat sauté magic. Because you are not using oil or butter to prevent food from sticking to the bottom of the pan, it helps to use nonstick sauté pans for these recipes.

tomato products

WHEN USING CANNED tomatoes (which is what I use most of the time, except in the summer, when plum tomatoes are at their best), I like to use whole, peeled plum tomatoes because they are closest in taste to fresh tomatoes. Little has been done to them, whereas canned or bottled purées, pastes, or sauces have a processed taste. Experiment with different brands available in your supermarket to find the brand you like best.

TILAPIA POMODORO

TILAPIA, A CENTRAL American white fish, comes from Costa Rica. Its taste is mild, but its most important attribute is its firmness, which helps it maintain its shape regardless of cooking method. Delicate fillets, such as flounder or sole, will fall apart in the cooking process. So if you can't get tilapia, choose among the many other varieties of firm, meaty fillets, such as catfish, sea bass, monkfish, snapper, salmon, etc. As long as the fish is not overly delicate, it will work fine in this recipe.

makes 2 servings

¾ cup fish broth

½ medium clove garlic, minced

Red pepper flakes to taste

2 tilapia fillets, about 8 ounces each

¼ cup medium-bodied red wine

2 cups plum tomatoes, cut in medium dice

Salt and freshly ground black pepper to taste

2 tablespoons basil leaves, sliced, plus 2 whole leaves, for garnish

2 cups rice or risotto, cooked according to package directions (see note)

Put ¼ cup of the fish broth in a large nonstick skillet over medium-high heat for 30 seconds. Sauté the garlic and pepper flakes in the hot broth for 30 seconds. Put the fish fillets and another ¼ cup of the fish broth in the skillet and cook for about 2 minutes, or until the liquid has almost evaporated and the bottom of the fish begins to brown slightly. Brown the second side of the fish for about 30 seconds more.

Add the wine and cook for another 30 seconds, until the wine begins to evaporate. Cook the tomatoes, salt, and pepper for about 30 seconds until the tomatoes begin to soften. Add the remaining ¼ cup of broth and cook for about 2 minutes more, until the fish turns opaque. Add a bit more broth, if needed, then the sliced basil. Remove from the heat.

To serve, spoon 1 cup of rice or risotto on each serving plate. Using a large spatula, place a fish fillet over each mound of rice or risotto, top with the tomato sauce, and garnish each plate with a basil leaf. Serve immediately.

NOTE: Risotto is made from a package of Arborio rice.

MIXED SEAFOOD RISOTTO

THIS DISH HAS been on my menu since 1995, and it's still a favorite. Even though it has almost no fat, it is totally satisfying. The seafood is poached in fish broth and stays plump and moist. The risotto is sautéed in tomato, fish broth, and a bit of White Wine Sauce, making it creamy and flavorful. You'll love this dish even if you aren't watching your fat intake.

makes 2 entrée or 4 first-course servings

SEAFOOD:

 1 1/4 cups fish broth

 1/2 medium clove garlic, minced

 Freshly ground black pepper, crushed red pepper flakes, and Old Bay seasoning
    to taste

 1/2 pound salmon fillet, skinned and cut into 4 pieces

 6 sea scallops

 1/4 cup white wine

 6 medium or large shrimp, shelled and deveined

 1 can artichoke hearts, packed in water and drained (see note)

 Salt and additional freshly ground black pepper to taste

RISOTTO:

 1/4 cup fish broth

 1/2 medium clove garlic, minced

 Black pepper and red pepper flakes to taste

 2 cups risotto, cooked according to directions on a package of Arborio rice but with
    about 5 minutes' less cooking time than called for

¼ cup White Wine Sauce (page 222)

1 cup Marinara Sauce (page 224)

2 tablespoons basil leaves, sliced

Salt to taste

2 tablespoons Italian (flat-leaf) parsley, stems removed and chopped

2 to 4 large basil leaves, for garnish

To make the seafood, put ¼ cup of the fish broth with the garlic, black pepper, red pepper flakes, and Old Bay in a large nonstick sauté pan over high heat and cook for 30 seconds. Add the salmon, scallops, and another ¼ cup of fish broth, and cook for 1 minute, until the liquid is almost gone and the fish just begins to brown. Turn the seafood, cook for 1 minute more, add the wine, and cook for another minute. Add another ½ cup of broth and reduce the heat to medium.

Cook for about 4 minutes (more or less, depending on the thickness of the fish), or until the salmon and the scallops turn completely opaque and almost all the liquid has evaporated. Cook the shrimp until they have begun to brown on both sides, about 1 minute per side. Add ¼ cup of broth and the artichokes, and cook until the shrimp turn pink on both sides, about 2 minutes. Remove from the heat and adjust the seasoning.

To make the risotto, put 2 tablespoons of the fish broth in another large nonstick sauté pan over high heat; add the garlic, black pepper, and red pepper flakes; and cook for 30 seconds. Add the risotto, the White Wine Sauce, and the Marinara Sauce. Stir continually while slowly adding the remaining 2 tablespoons of fish broth. Cook until all the liquid is absorbed and the risotto is heated thoroughly. Stir in the sliced basil, remove from the heat, and season with the salt.

To serve, divide the risotto among individual serving plates, top with the seafood, sprinkle with parsley, and garnish with a basil leaf.

NOTE: Artichokes are usually sold in 14-ounce cans that yield about 8½ ounces after draining.

PESTO FETTUCCINE WITH RED BELL PEPPERS AND SUN-DRIED TOMATOES

THIS DISH USES a pesto sauce made with chicken broth instead of oil, and it's combined with some White Wine Sauce for creaminess. This sauce hugs the fettuccine and makes you feel as if you are eating something rich and fattening, even though the only fat in this dish is the very small amount from the White Wine Sauce.

makes 3 entrée or 8 first-course servings

1 pound fettuccine

¾ cup chicken broth

1 small clove garlic, minced

Pinch of red pepper flakes

1 red bell pepper, cut into ¼-inch strips

1 cup White Wine Sauce (page 222)

¼ cup dry-packed sun-dried tomatoes, slivered

1 cup Low-Fat Pesto Sauce (recipe follows) or standard Pesto Sauce (page 115 or store-bought), excess oil removed

3 to 6 fresh basil leaves or 4 radicchio leaves (for garnish)

Cook the pasta according to package directions in a large pot of boiling, salted water. While the pasta cooks, put ¼ cup of the chicken broth in a medium nonstick sauté pan over high heat and cook the garlic and red pepper flakes in the broth for 30 seconds. Sauté the pepper strips and the remaining chicken broth for 1 to 2 minutes, until the peppers begin to soften and turn brown and the broth has almost evaporated. Add the White Wine Sauce, sun-dried tomatoes, and Low-Fat Pesto Sauce, stir, and cook for about 3 minutes, or until the peppers are soft but still slightly crunchy and the sauce comes to a boil. Reduce the heat and simmer for another minute. The sauce will also thicken during this time; add a bit more broth if it is too thick. Remove from the heat.

To serve, drain the pasta and toss it in a large serving bowl with half the liquid portion of the sauce. Divide the pasta among individual serving plates and top each serving with additional sauce and some peppers. Garnish with a basil leaf or a red radicchio leaf for contrasting color.

LOW-FAT PESTO SAUCE

Makes about 1 cup

1 cup basil leaves, loosely packed

1 cup Italian (flat-leaf) parsley leaves, loosely packed

½ cup chicken broth or vegetable broth

¼ cup pine nuts (optional)

2 medium cloves garlic

⅓ cup freshly grated Parmesan or Romano cheese (optional)

Salt to taste

Put the basil, parsley, broth, pine nuts, and garlic in the workbowl of a food processor and process until smooth. Pour the sauce into a bowl, stir in the cheese, and add salt. Use as directed in the previous recipe.

SHRIMP, SPINACH, AND ARTICHOKES OVER LINGUINE

ANY TIME I create a recipe, I look for flavors and ingredients that complement each other. No single ingredient overwhelms any other unless it is intended to take center stage. In pasta dishes, the pasta itself must be able to stand up to the sauce. In this dish, all ingredients are in harmony. You can taste every flavor. The added bonus is that it looks good, too. Even the colors complement each other. Instead of shrimp, feel free to use scallops, lobster meat, or even chunks of salmon.

makes 4 servings

1 pound linguine or other long, thin pasta

½ cup fish broth

½ medium clove garlic, minced

Pinch of red pepper flakes

2 dozen medium shrimp, cleaned and deveined

1 can artichoke hearts (see note)

¼ cup white wine

½ cup black olives, pitted and sliced

1 bag (10 ounces) fresh spinach

2 cups White Wine Sauce (page 222)

Salt and freshly ground black pepper to taste

Basil leaves (for garnish)

Radicchio leaves (for garnish)

Cook the pasta according to package directions in a large pot of boiling, salted water.

While the pasta cooks, put half the fish broth, the garlic, red pepper flakes, shrimp, and artichoke hearts in a medium nonstick sauté pan over high heat. Cook for about 1 minute, until the shrimp and artichoke hearts begin to turn slightly brown and the broth has almost evaporated. Turn the shrimp and the artichokes, add the wine, cook for another 30 seconds, and add the olives, spinach, White Wine Sauce, and remaining fish broth.

Cook and stir for about 2 minutes, or until the shrimp are opaque and the sauce comes to a boil. Remove from the heat and season with salt and pepper.

To serve, drain the pasta and toss it in a large serving bowl with half the sauce. Top with the remaining sauce, then divide among individual serving plates and top each serving with the shrimp and other ingredients. Garnish each plate with a basil leaf or a red radicchio leaf for contrasting color.

NOTE: Artichokes are usually sold in 14-ounce cans that yield about 8½ ounces after draining.

CHICKEN, STRING BEANS, AND TOMATOES OVER SPAGHETTI

C HICKEN ALWAYS ADDS wonderful flavor to any dish and it's naturally low in fat, especially the breast. Add fresh string beans and tomatoes and you can't help but pack in the flavor. In this recipe, I use bits of fresh tomato as an ingredient, not as the base of the sauce. The base is the White Wine Sauce. It's yet another example of a recipe in which the flavors of all the ingredients can be tasted through the subtlety of this versatile sauce.

makes 4 servings

1 pound spaghetti

1 medium clove garlic, minced

Pinch of red pepper flakes

¾ cup chicken broth

1 boneless chicken breast, split, cut into ½-inch strips and dredged in seasoned flour

½ pound string beans, ends removed

4 plum tomatoes, cut in medium dice

¼ cup white wine

2 cups White Wine Sauce (page 222)

Salt and freshly ground black pepper to taste

Basil leaves, for garnish

Radicchio leaves, for garnish

Cook the pasta according to package directions in a large pot of boiling, salted water. While the pasta cooks, sauté the garlic and the red pepper flakes with ¼ cup of the chicken broth in a medium, nonstick sauté pan over high heat for 30 seconds. Add another ¼ cup of broth with the chicken and string beans, and cook for about 2 minutes, until most of the broth has evaporated and the beans and chicken begin to brown slightly on one side. Turn the chicken and stir the string beans, add the tomatoes, and cook for another minute, giving the tomatoes a chance to sauté and the second side of the chicken to brown.

Add the wine, cook for 1 minute, and add the White Wine Sauce and the remaining broth. Stir and cook for about 3 minutes, until the chicken is completely opaque and cooked thoroughly and the sauce comes to a boil. Reduce the heat and simmer 1 minute more. The sauce will reduce and thicken during this time. Add more broth if it is too thick. Remove from the heat and season with salt and pepper.

To serve, drain the pasta and toss it in a large serving bowl with half the liquid portion of the sauce. Divide the pasta among individual serving plates and top with the remaining sauce liquid, chicken, and other ingredients. Garnish each plate with a basil leaf or a red radicchio leaf for contrasting color.

CHICKEN IN A TOMATO PESTO SAUCE OVER LINGUINE

T HIS DISH BRINGS together three delicious flavors: chicken, tomatoes, and pesto. Combining tomato and pesto sauces works wonderfully because the tomato sauce is a perfect balance for the intensity of the pesto. Think about it. Pesto is made with herbs and Parmesan, both of which we'd probably add to our tomato sauce anyway. It makes perfect sense to combine the two. Even a low-fat pesto added to tomato sauce simply intensifies the flavor of the herbs. The chicken adds yet another dimension to the sauce, and the result is simply delicious. For this recipe, the tomato sauce is my standard marinara.

makes 4 servings

1 pound linguine
¾ cup chicken broth
1 medium clove garlic, minced
Pinch of red pepper flakes
1 boneless chicken breast, split, cut into ½-inch strips and dredged in seasoned flour
2 cups Marinara Sauce (page 224)
½ cup Low-Fat Pesto Sauce (page 145) (see note)
Salt and freshly ground black pepper to taste
Basil or radicchio leaves (for garnish)

Cook the pasta according to package directions in a large pot of boiling, salted water. Cook ¼ cup of the chicken broth, the garlic, and the red pepper flakes in a large nonstick sauté pan over high heat for 30 seconds. Add another ¼ cup of chicken broth and cook the chicken strips for about 2 minutes, until most of the broth has evaporated

150

and the chicken has begun to brown slightly. Turn the chicken, add the remaining broth, and cook for another minute or so, until the chicken browns on the second side.

Add the Marinara Sauce and Low-Fat Pesto Sauce, stir, and cook for about 2 minutes, until the chicken is completely opaque and cooked thoroughly and the sauce comes to a boil. Reduce the heat and simmer for 1 minute more. The sauce will reduce and thicken during this time. Add more broth if it is too thick. Remove from the heat and season with the salt and pepper.

To serve, drain the pasta and toss it in a large serving bowl with half the liquid portion of the sauce. Divide the pasta among individual serving plates and top each serving with some of the remaining liquid sauce and a portion of the chicken. Garnish with a basil leaf or a red radicchio leaf for contrasting color. Adjust seasoning and serve.

NOTE: If you want to use a regular pesto sauce, see page 115.

PAN-SEARED TUNA PUTTANESCA

T O MAKE ANY dish delicious, you must start with the freshest ingredients you can find, especially when cooking without fat, which we all know add tons of flavor. Take away the fat and we have to get our flavor from the ingredients themselves. This dish is a perfect example of how to do just that. Fresh tuna is delicious to begin with, so there's no need to add much. Combine it with ripe tomatoes and flavorful kalamata olives and capers, and you won't miss the fat at all.

makes 4 servings

4 tuna steaks, about 8 ounces each, dredged in ½ cup seasoned flour

½ cup fish broth

Pinch of red pepper flakes

Salt and freshly ground black pepper to taste

½ medium clove garlic, minced

12 fresh plum tomatoes, cut in medium dice

¼ cup chopped kalamata olives

2 tablespoons capers, drained

¼ cup Marinara Sauce (page 224)

1 tablespoon Italian (flat-leaf) parsley, stems removed and chopped

4 to 6 fresh basil leaves, slivered (for garnish)

Preheat the oven to 200°F. Dredge the tuna steaks in the flour, and shake off any excess.

Cook half the fish broth with the red pepper flakes in a large nonstick sauté pan over high heat, for about 30 seconds. Place the tuna steaks in the hot broth, and cook for about 1 minute per side for medium-rare. Remove the cooked steaks from the pan, season with the salt and pepper, and keep them warm in the oven.

Cook the garlic in the pan for about 30 seconds, until it just begins to turn golden brown, and add the tomatoes, olives, and capers. Cook for about 30 seconds, and add the remaining broth and Marinara Sauce. Cook for about 1 minute more, or until the tomatoes begin to soften and the sauce begins to boil. Remove from the heat, and season with additional salt and pepper.

To serve, put the sauce on a warm platter or individual plates, place the tuna on top of the sauce, sprinkle with parsley, and garnish with the basil.

153

CHICKEN POMODORO OVER LINGUINE

W HENEVER YOU WANT a low-fat dish of pasta, reach for a bunch of ripe plum tomatoes or a can of whole peeled plum tomatoes. You can then sauté some spices in a little broth, cook the tomatoes, toss them with the pasta, and top it off with some fresh basil or parsley. In less than 20 minutes, start to finish, you'll have a satisfying dish. To make it more interesting, first sauté pieces of chicken, fish, or vegetables. With this simple method, you can come up with an almost endless variety of low-fat dishes. In this recipe, I use strips of chicken breast to flavor my tomato sauce. Even though the breast is the least fatty part of the chicken, it adds wonderful flavor.

makes 4 servings

1 pound linguine

1 cup chicken broth

½ medium clove garlic, minced

Pinch of red pepper flakes

1 boneless chicken breast, split, cut into ½-inch strips and dredged in seasoned flour

6 to 8 fresh plum tomatoes, diced, or 1 can (28 ounces) diced plum tomatoes

¼ cup Marinara Sauce (page 224)

Salt and freshly ground black pepper to taste

4 or 5 basil leaves, sliced

Cook the pasta according to package directions in a large pot of boiling, salted water.
Cook ¼ cup of the chicken broth, the garlic, and the red pepper flakes in a large nonstick sauté pan over high heat for 30 seconds. Add another ¼ cup of chicken broth and the chicken strips, and cook for about 2 minutes, until most of the broth has

evaporated and the chicken begins to turn slightly brown on one side. Turn the chicken, add another ¼ cup of broth, and cook for another minute or so, until the second side of the chicken browns and, again, the broth has nearly evaporated.

Sauté the tomatoes for 1 minute, or until they begin to soften and release their juices, then add the Marinara Sauce and the remaining broth, and cook for about 3 minutes or until the chicken is completely opaque and cooked thoroughly and the sauce comes to a boil. Remove from the heat and season with the salt and pepper.

To serve, drain the pasta and toss it in a large serving bowl with half the liquid sauce. Divide the pasta among individual serving plates and top each serving with some of the remaining sauce and the chicken pieces. Adjust the seasoning, garnish with the basil, and serve immediately.

SHRIMP OVER SPAGHETTI POMODORO

T HIS RECIPE IS a variation on the previous recipe, Chicken Pomodoro with Linguine. Here, though, fish broth is used to sauté the shrimp rather than chicken broth to sauté chicken. The flavor is totally different but the method is the same. The sauce for this dish can be made in the time it takes to cook the pasta.

makes 4 servings

1 pound linguine

½ cup fish broth

Pinch of red pepper flakes

1 pound medium or large shrimp, cleaned and deveined

½ medium clove garlic, minced

6 to 8 fresh plum tomatoes, diced, or 1 can (28 ounces) diced plum tomatoes

¼ cup Marinara Sauce (page 224)

Salt and freshly ground black pepper to taste

4 or 5 basil leaves, sliced

Cook the pasta according to package directions in a large pot of boiling, salted water.

Cook half the fish broth and the red pepper flakes in a large nonstick sauté pan over high heat for about 30 seconds. Sauté the shrimp in the hot liquid for about 30 seconds on each side, or just until the shrimp begins to turn pink. Add the garlic and cook for 30 seconds more. Add the diced tomatoes and cook for about 30 seconds.

Cook the Marinara Sauce and the remaining fish broth. Stir for another minute, until the shrimp are opaque and the tomatoes have softened. Remove from the heat and season with the salt and pepper.

To serve, drain the pasta, transfer it to a large serving bowl, and toss it with half the liquid portion of the sauce. Divide the pasta among individual serving plates and top each serving with additional liquid. Arrange the shrimp over each serving, and garnish with the basil.

LOW-FAT RICOTTA AND BASIL
OVER PENNE MARINARA

T HIS DISH IS made using the basic Marinara Sauce on page 224. Although this recipe uses oil to sauté the onions and garlic, the amount per serving is tiny, so you get a lot of bang for your buck. However, if you need to be truly stringent on your fat content, go ahead and substitute chicken broth or vegetable broth for the oil. The low-fat ricotta melts into the hot sauce and coats the penne, adding a delightfully deceiving richness to this dish.

158

makes 4 servings

1 pound penne pasta

2 tablespoons extra virgin olive oil

Pinch of red pepper flakes

½ medium clove garlic, minced

2 cups Marinara Sauce (page 224)

¼ cup chicken broth

Salt and freshly ground black pepper to taste

1 container (16 ounces) low-fat ricotta cheese

1 tablespoon Italian (flat-leaf) parsley, stems removed and chopped

4 or 5 fresh basil leaves, slivered (for garnish)

Cook the pasta according to package directions in a large pot of boiling, salted water.
Heat the oil and red pepper flakes in a large nonstick sauté pan over high heat for about 30 seconds. Sauté the garlic for 30 seconds more, or until the garlic begins to turn golden, then add the Marinara Sauce and the chicken broth and cook for about 2 minutes, or until the sauce starts to boil. Remove from the heat and season with salt and pepper.

To serve, drain the pasta and toss it in a large serving bowl with half the liquid portion of the sauce. Divide the pasta among individual serving plates. Top each serving with additional sauce, dot with the ricotta, sprinkle with parsley, and garnish with basil.

ROASTED VEGETABLES OVER PENNE

THIS DISH HAS been on my fat-free menu at Biscotti for years. It's a favorite. Fresh vegetables, such as eggplant, zucchini, fennel, carrots, or bell peppers, are thinly sliced and roasted on a sheet pan under your broiler. The vegetables cook in their own juices with no added oil, which you would have to use if you were to grill them. We then sauté a quick tomato sauce, toss it with the penne, and lay all those delicious fresh vegetables over the pasta. It's beautiful, delicious, and very healthy, especially if you pick the vegetables from your garden or buy them from a farmer's market.

makes 4 servings

Vegetable spray

1 firm medium-sized eggplant, cut in ¼-inch horizontal slices

1 firm medium-sized zucchini, cut in ¼-inch horizontal slices

2 large red bell peppers, cut in ½-inch slices

2 large carrots, sliced ¼ inch thick

1 large yellow onion, cut in ½-inch circles

1 fennel bulb, sliced ½ inch thick

Salt and freshly ground black pepper to taste

1 pound penne pasta

¼ cup vegetable or chicken broth

Pinch of red pepper flakes

1 medium clove garlic, minced

3 cups Marinara Sauce (page 224)

3 or 4 basil leaves, slivered

While the pasta water comes to a boil, roast the vegetables. Spray a large baking sheet with a vegetable spray, such as Pam. After the eggplant, zucchini, bell peppers, carrots, onion, and fennel are sliced, put as many varieties as possible on the baking sheet in a single layer, sprinkle the vegetables with the salt and pepper, and put the sheet under the broiler, about 4 to 5 inches from the source of the heat.

Check the tray after 1 minute and turn any slices that have turned brown. As the vegetables brown on both sides and soften, remove them and pile them on a large platter, with each variety in its own pile. Replace each empty spot on the baking sheet with a new pile of raw vegetables. When all the vegetables have been roasted and transferred to a platter, cover the platter with plastic wrap (this will soften them further and keep them warm) and set aside.

Cook the pasta according to package directions in a large pot of boiling, salted water.

While the pasta cooks, put the broth and the red pepper flakes in a large nonstick skillet over high heat and cook for 30 seconds. Sauté the garlic for about 30 seconds, or just until it begins to turn golden. Add the Marinara Sauce and cook for about 2 minutes, until the sauce begins to boil. Remove from the heat and season with salt and pepper.

To serve, drain the pasta and transfer it to a large bowl. Toss with half the sauce, put the pasta on individual serving plates, and top with the remaining sauce. Top the pasta servings with each variety of the roasted vegetables until the surface of the pasta is completely covered. Garnish with the basil.

7

SAUTÉ pizza

WHEN I WAS a student living in Ravenna, Italy, in 1975 and 1976, I would spend as many weekends as I could in Florence, a two-hour train ride away. The first time I visited this beautiful city, I was reading Irving Stone's *The Agony and the Ecstasy*, a novel based on the life of Michelangelo. I spent a lot of time sitting on the steps of the *duomo* where Michelangelo and Leonardo da Vinci had sat 500 years earlier contemplating the universe. I felt such a connection.

What does all that have to do with pizza? Well, with all the wonders of Florence, the wonders of its pizza did not escape me. Since I could rarely afford a meal in a restaurant, I ate a lot of pizza, and I never grew tired of it. In Florence, even pizza was a work of art.

Prominently displayed in the windows of countless shops were squares of this classic dish, topped with everything imaginable: exotic mushrooms, broccoli rabe, zucchini, roasted peppers, calamari, and more. I had never seen any pizza toppings in the States beyond cheese, pepperoni, sausage, and canned mushrooms. America was still years away from discovering gourmet pizza. Once we did, we ran with it, reinventing pizza in characteristic American style that would have the Italians turning up their noses at the ridiculousness of putting such things as pineapple, salad greens, or even pasta on pizza!

Still, as with anything else, there is always room for something new.

For me, sauté and pizza go together like the proverbial horse and carriage. Just imagine how much more flavorful a pizza could be if the toppings were sautéed in interesting combinations instead of just plopped on raw or boiled! You are about to find out. Enjoy.

Some Things You Should Know

- All the toppings in this chapter's recipes are intended for two medium-sized pizzas (each about 12 inches in diameter).
- For all the pizza recipes below, pre-baked crusts may be substituted for crusts you make from scratch or for purchased pizza dough. I have tested all three methods. All work well, so use what's best for you. I find that starting with a batch of fresh, premade dough is the quickest, easiest way of getting the type of crust I like. I can mold the dough to whatever thickness and size I want, and, with a bit of experimenting with my oven temperature, I can get the degree of crispness I desire. Many supermarkets carry pizza or bread dough. If you can't find it at your local market, try asking at your local pizza shop whether you may purchase some. Most will be happy to oblige. If you are someone who makes bread or would like to, pizza dough is made the same way. It's not difficult. Just allow a few hours to let the dough rise. We make our own bread at the restaurant every day. When I want to make pizza, I simply put some dough aside for this purpose.

- Play around with shaping the dough and getting it to your desired thickness. Overworking the dough will make it too tough. But practice will give you a better result, so have some extra dough and a little patience on hand.

- Though thin-crust pizzas seem to be all the rage at the moment, keep in mind that a very thin crust is not always best, especially with heavier toppings or sauces. A thin crust is best when using a very thin tomato sauce or no sauce at all, just fresh sliced ingredients or cheese. But for most of the recipes in this chapter, a slightly thicker crust is better. Keep in mind, though, that pizza dough will almost double its original thickness in the oven. I find that starting with pizza dough that is rolled or worked into shape and is about $\frac{1}{4}$ inch thick is ideal for these recipes.

- After making a couple of the recipes below, you will find that there is almost a formula to this. Simply plug in your favorite ingredients and go.

grilled pizza

DID YOU KNOW that you can make a superb pizza crust right on your grill? This is a featured specialty in my grilling class—and the raves are music to my ears—especially when they include those of my teenage son, Mathew.

Simply make the dough as I've described in this chapter, place it on a medium hot, well-oiled grill (charcoal or gas), cook for about 3 to 4 minutes, or until the underside is firm, and flip. Wow! A beautiful crust, and grill lines too! Top with your favorite sauce, followed by the cheese of your choice, and cook for an additional 3 to 4 minutes. Cover if necessary. Make one for your whole family and have a party!

BASIC PIZZA DOUGH

P|LAY WITH THIS dough! This is where you get to determine how thick your crust will be and how good you are at making circles. (Remember, the dough will thicken as it bakes in the oven.) Your first attempts always come out looking like amoeba, or you stretch the dough so thin in certain spots that you get holes in the dough. Don't fret. It gets easier with a little practice. Doesn't everything?

makes 2 round pies, each 8 to 10 inches in diameter, or 1 rectangular pie, about 10 x 14 inches. (This recipe can easily be doubled, tripled, or more.)

1 teaspoon (slightly heaping) active dry yeast

¾ cup warm (not hot) water, approximately

3 cups unbleached white flour

1 teaspoon salt

Combine the yeast and ¼ cup of the warm water in a small mixing bowl. Set aside until frothy, about 10 to 15 minutes.

Put the flour in a large mixing bowl and make a well in the center. Put the frothy yeast liquid, the remaining water, and the salt in the well, and combine until all the flour is incorporated into a dough ball. If a bit of flour remains loose, add a few drops of water at a time until all the flour is mixed into the ball of dough. If it becomes too sticky, mix in a small handful of flour. Cover with plastic wrap and leave at room temperature for about an hour or so, or until the dough has doubled in size and is light and airy.

Transfer the dough to a floured board or surface, punch your fist into the center of the dough to deflate it, and divide the dough in half. Cover one of the halves with a large bowl, and set it aside while you work with the other half.

Shape the dough into a circle by pushing out from the center with your knuckles. Keep working the dough, flattening it until you have a circle about ¼ inch thick and 8 to 10 inches in diameter. Repeat with the second piece of dough. Use as directed in any of the recipes in this chapter.

PIZZA CACCIATORA

WHEN I WAS growing up, chicken cacciatora was one of my favorite dishes. The juices from the chicken add such wonderful flavor to any tomato sauce. My mother would brown chicken thighs and legs in a large stockpot, add canned tomatoes, and simmer the sauce until the chicken pieces were almost falling off the bone. That's when she would transfer the chicken to a serving platter. The chicken-infused tomato sauce would be tossed over pasta and sprinkled with Parmesan cheese. This was a traditional Thursday night meal in my house. In this recipe, I make chicken cacciatora by using boneless chicken breasts because they are so adaptable to sauté and perfect for a pizza topping. The chicken, lightly browned in the sauté pan and cooked in the Marinara Sauce, takes just minutes to prepare. Placing it on your pizza crust and topping it with fresh mozzarella is all that's needed to bring these wonderful flavors to your table.

makes 2 pizzas, each 8 to 10 inches in diameter

Dough from Basic Pizza Dough recipe (page 168),
  or 2 premade 8- to 10-inch pizza crusts

2 tablespoons extra virgin olive oil

Pinch of red pepper flakes

1/2 pound boneless chicken breast, cut into 1/4-inch strips and
  dredged in seasoned flour

1 medium clove garlic, minced

2 to 3 tablespoons chicken broth

1 cup Marinara Sauce (page 224)

Salt and freshly ground black pepper to taste

½ pound fresh mozzarella, shredded, approximately

1 tablespoon Italian (flat-leaf) parsley, or basil, thinly sliced

Preheat the oven to 400°F. Shape the dough as desired and place it on a greased baking sheet.

Put the oil and red pepper flakes in a large sauté pan over high heat for about 30 seconds, or until the oil is hot but not smoking. Add the chicken pieces and cook for about 1 minute, or until the chicken begins to brown. Turn the chicken strips and add the garlic. Cook briefly, until the garlic starts to turn golden brown, and add the broth and the Marinara Sauce. Stir and cook for about 3 minutes, until the sauce is reduced and has thickened. If the sauce looks too thick and dry, add a bit more broth. Remove the pan from the heat and season with salt and pepper.

Divide the contents of the sauté pan onto each crust and bake the pizza in the preheated oven for 10 minutes. Remove the pizzas from the oven and dot each with as little or as much mozzarella as you like. Return the pizza to the oven for about 10 more minutes, until the bottom of the crust has browned and the cheese has melted. Remove from the oven, sprinkle with fresh parsley or basil, cut into slices, and serve.

PIZZA POMODORO WITH ARUGULA

T HIS IS A twist on the classic margarita pizza, which is topped with fresh tomatoes, mozzarella, and basil. Arugula is a delicate, deeply notched green leaf about 2 to 3 inches long with a distinctive spicy, peppery taste. It is used in salads and sauces, or, in this case, is sliced and used to top pizza. Italians have always loved it, and now Americans love it too.

makes 2 pizzas, each 8 to 10 inches in diameter

Dough from Basic Pizza Dough recipe (page 168), or 2 premade 8- to 10-inch crusts

2 to 3 tablespoons extra-virgin olive oil

Pinch of red pepper flakes

6 plum tomatoes, cut in medium dice

½ small clove garlic, minced

2 to 3 tablespoons chicken broth

2 to 3 tablespoons Marinara Sauce (page 224)

Salt and freshly ground black pepper to taste

½ pound fresh mozzarella, shredded

5 or 6 fresh arugula leaves, cut into ¼-inch-wide strips

Preheat the oven to 400°F. Shape the dough as desired and place it on a greased baking sheet.

Put the oil and the red pepper flakes in a large sauté pan over high heat for about 30 seconds, or until the oil is hot but not smoking. Sauté the tomatoes for about 30 seconds, or until they just begin to soften. Cook the garlic briefly, just until it begins to turn golden. Add the broth and the Marinara Sauce, stir, and cook for about 1 minute more, or until the sauce just begins to boil. Remove the pan from the heat and season with the salt and pepper.

Divide the contents of the sauté pan onto each crust. Bake for about 10 minutes. Remove the pizzas from the oven, and dot each with as little or as much mozzarella cheese as you like. Return the pizzas to the oven for approximately 10 minutes, or until the bottoms are brown and the cheese has melted. Remove from the oven, sprinkle with the arugula, cut in slices, and serve.

173

PIZZA WITH TOMATO-PESTO AND GOAT CHEESE

T HIS SIMPLE SAUCE alone makes this a memorable pizza. For lovers of goat cheese, this pizza is irresistible. For others, substitute ricotta or mozzarella.

makes 2 pizzas, each 8 to 10 inches in diameter

Dough from Basic Pizza Dough recipe (page 168),
 or 2 premade 8- to 10-inch crusts

2 tablespoons extra virgin olive oil

Pinch of red pepper flakes

1 medium clove garlic, minced

1/2 cup Marinara Sauce (page 224)

1/4 cup Pesto Sauce (page 115)

2 to 3 tablespoons chicken broth (optional)

Salt and freshly ground black pepper to taste

6 ounces goat cheese, approximately (see note)

5 or 6 leaves basil leaves, cut into 1/4-inch strips

Preheat the oven to 400°F. Shape the dough as desired and place it on a greased baking sheet.

Put the oil, red pepper flakes, and garlic in a large sauté pan over high heat for about 30 seconds, or just until the garlic begins to turn golden brown. Add the Marinara Sauce and Pesto Sauce, stir, and cook for about 1 minute, until the sauce begins to boil. If the sauce looks too thick, add the chicken broth. Remove from heat and season with the salt and pepper.

Divide the contents of the sauté pan onto each crust and bake for 10 minutes. Remove the pizzas from the oven and dot each with as little or as much goat cheese as you like. Return the pizzas to the oven for about 10 minutes, or until the bottoms of the crusts have browned and the cheese has melted. Remove the pies from the oven, cut into slices, sprinkle with the basil, and serve.

175

PIZZA WITH SHELLFISH AND TOMATOES

I LIKE TO make this pizza with Manila clams and Prince Edward Island mussels, not only because I like both but also because both have similar cooking times, so you don't have to worry about overcooking one while undercooking the other. This pizza is a showstopper.

makes 2 pizzas, each 8 to 10 inches in diameter

Dough from Basic Pizza Dough recipe (page 168),
   or 2 premade 8- to 10-inch crusts
2 tablespoons extra virgin olive oil
Pinch of red pepper flakes
2 to 3 anchovy fillets, chopped (optional)
1 dozen Manila clams (see note)
1 dozen Prince Edward Island mussels (see note)
1 medium clove garlic, minced
1 cup Marinara Sauce (page 224)
2 to 3 tablespoons bottled clam juice
Freshly ground black pepper to taste
5 or 6 basil leaves, cut into ¼-inch strips

Preheat the oven to 400°F. Shape the dough as desired and place it on a greased baking sheet.

Cook the oil, red pepper flakes, and anchovy in a large sauté pan over high heat for about 30 seconds, or until the oil is hot but not smoking. Cook the clams and mussels for 1 to 2 minutes, or until the shells just begin to open. Sauté the garlic for a few seconds, until it begins to turn golden brown. Add the Marinara Sauce and the clam juice, stir, and cook for about 1 minute, until the sauce begins to boil. Remove from the heat and season with the black pepper.

Divide the contents of the sauté pan onto each pizza crust, and bake for about 15 to 20 minutes, or until the bottom of the crust is brown and crispy. Remove from the oven, cut into slices, sprinkle with the basil, and serve.

NOTE: Top the pizza with the clams and mussels still in their shells because it looks so appealing. Be sure to put an empty bowl on the table so the shells can be placed in it as the pizza is eaten.

PIZZA PUTTANESCA
WITH ASIAGO CHEESE

P UTTANESCA ORIGINATED IN southern Italy under some very humble conditions. Local myth tells of how the "ladies of the night" were not allowed to shop until "respectable" patrons had left the store. Naturally, they were left with very little to choose from. So taking what was left, they made a sauce with a little anchovy, some tomatoes, a few olives, and capers and tossed it over pasta. As it turned out, the result—among the very best of the red sauces—is now considered a classic. The recipe below is just as delicious over pasta as over pizza.

makes 2 pizzas, each 8 to 10 inches in diameter

Dough from Basic Pizza Dough recipe (page 168), or 2 premade 8- to 10-inch crusts

2 tablespoons extra virgin olive oil

Pinch of red pepper flakes

2 to 3 anchovy fillets, chopped

1 medium clove garlic, minced

½ cup Marinara Sauce (page 224)

¼ cup kalamata olives (or other favorite), pitted

2 tablespoons capers, drained

2 to 3 tablespoons chicken broth

Salt and freshly ground black pepper to taste

Approximately ¼ cup Asiago cheese (or Parmesan, or Romano), shredded

5 or 6 basil leaves, cut into ¼-inch strips

Preheat the oven to 400°F. Shape the dough as desired and place it on a greased baking sheet.

SIMPLY **sauté**

Cook the oil, red pepper flakes, anchovy, and garlic in a large sauté pan over high heat for a few moments, until the garlic begins to turn golden brown. Add the Marinara Sauce, olives, capers, and chicken broth, and cook for about 1 minute, until the sauce begins to boil. If the sauce looks too thick and dry, add a bit more broth. Remove from the heat and season with the salt and pepper.

Divide the contents of the sauté pan between each crust, bake for about 10 minutes, remove the pizzas from the oven, and dot each with as little or as much cheese as you like. Return the pizzas to the oven for about 10 minutes, until the bottoms of the crusts have browned and the cheese has melted. Remove the pizzas from the oven, sprinkle with the basil, cut into slices, and serve.

PIZZA WITH EGGPLANT, TOMATOES, AND SMOKED MOZZARELLA

EGGPLANT IS A favorite ingredient in southern Italian cooking. When cooked properly, it is truly delicious. But if the slices are too thick or if they're not allowed cooked thoroughly, the eggplant will be bitter and unappealing. Once you try sautéing it, you'll get hooked on eggplant, even if you thought you didn't like it.

makes 2 pizzas, each 8 to 10 inches in diameter

Dough from Basic Pizza Dough recipe (page 168), or 2 premade 8- to 10-inch crusts

2 tablespoons extra virgin olive oil

Pinch of red pepper flakes

½ medium clove garlic, minced

1 eggplant, core removed, cut in medium dice

6 plum tomatoes, cut in medium dice

2 to 3 tablespoons chicken broth

¼ cup Marinara Sauce (page 224)

Salt and freshly ground black pepper to taste

Approximately ½ cup smoked mozzarella, cut in medium dice

5 or 6 basil leaves, cut into ¼-inch strips

Preheat the oven to 400°F. Shape the dough as desired and place it on a greased baking sheet.

Cook the oil, red pepper flakes, and garlic in a large sauté pan over high heat for about 30 seconds, until the garlic starts to turn golden brown. Cook the eggplant dice for about 2 minutes, until they begin to brown and soften, then cook the tomatoes for about 30 seconds, until they release their juices and begin to soften. Add the broth and the Marinara Sauce, stir, and cook for 1 more minute, until the sauce begins to boil. Remove from the heat and season with the salt and pepper.

Divide the contents of the sauté pan between the two crusts and bake them for 10 minutes. Remove the pizzas from the oven and dot each with as little or as much mozzarella as you like. Return them to the oven for about 10 minutes, or until the bottoms of the crusts have browned and the cheese has melted. Remove pizzas from the oven, cut into slices, sprinkle with basil, and serve.

PIZZA WITH
ANCHOVIES AND TOMATOES

Anchovies get a bad rap. Most people are so turned off by the way they look that they won't even try them. Yet, anchovies are so flavorful. I can't understand how anyone could dislike them. Most of the time, a bit of anchovy added to a recipe will go unnoticed but will do so much to flavor a sauce or dish. But this recipe is a different story. You must be an anchovy lover to love this pizza.

makes 2 pizzas, each 8 to 10 inches in diameter

Dough from Basic Pizza Dough recipe (page 168), or 2 premade 8- to 10-inch crusts

4 to 5 tablespoons extra virgin olive oil

1 medium clove garlic, minced

Pinch of red pepper flakes

8 to 10 anchovies, chopped

4 to 5 plum tomatoes, diced

½ cup Marinara Sauce (page 224)

2 to 3 tablespoons fish broth

Freshly ground black pepper to taste

4 or 5 leaves fresh basil, chopped

Preheat the oven to 400°F. Shape the dough as desired and place it on a greased baking sheet.

Put the oil in a large sauté pan over high heat for about 30 seconds, or until the oil is hot but not smoking. Sauté the garlic, red pepper flakes, and anchovies in the hot oil for 15 seconds, add the tomatoes, and cook for 30 seconds, until the tomatoes release their juices and begin to soften. Add the Marinara Sauce and the broth, stir, and cook for about 1 minute, or until the sauce begins to boil. Remove from the heat and season with the black pepper.

Divide the contents of the sauté pan between the two pizza crusts and bake for 15 to 20 minutes, or until the bottoms of the crusts are brown and crispy. Remove the pizzas from the oven, sprinkle with basil, cut into slices, and serve.

PIZZA WITH SAUTÉED ARTICHOKES, TOMATOES, BÉCHAMEL, AND RICOTTA

I F YOU *DON'T* like a lot of tomato sauce on your pizza and you *do* like artichokes, this is the pizza for you. Béchamel, a basic white sauce, when mixed with ricotta results in a creamy textured "cheese" that is a pleasant change from mozzarella.

makes 2 pizzas, each 8 to 10 inches in diameter

Dough from Basic Pizza Dough recipe (page 168), or 2 premade 8- to 10-inch crusts

3 to 4 tablespoons extra virgin olive oil

½ small clove garlic, minced

1 can artichoke hearts, packed in water, drained (see note)

2 plum tomatoes, diced

Salt and freshly ground black pepper to taste

1 cup Ricotta/Béchamel Sauce (page 84) (chilled for ½ hour, or until firm)

1 tablespoon Italian (flat-leaf) parsley, stems removed and chopped

Preheat the oven to 400°F. Shape the dough as desired and place it on a greased baking sheet.

Cook the oil and the garlic in a large sauté pan over high heat for about 30 seconds, until the garlic begins to turn golden brown. Cook the artichokes for about 30 seconds, until they begin to brown, then the tomatoes for another 30 seconds, until they begin to soften and release their juices. Remove from the heat and season with the salt and pepper.

Divide the contents of the sauté pan between the two pizza crusts and bake for 10 minutes. Remove the pizzas from the oven and dot each with several dollops of the ricotta/béchamel sauce. Return the pizzas to the oven for about 10 minutes, or until the bottoms of the crusts have browned and the cheese has melted. Remove the pizzas from the oven, sprinkle with the parsley, cut into slices, and serve.

NOTE: Artichokes are usually sold in 14-ounce cans that yield about 8½ ounces after draining.

PIZZA BOLOGNESE

THIS RECIPE FEATURES a classic Italian pasta meat sauce that's delicious on pizza. I like to use a combination of pork and turkey. The pork gives it a lot of flavor, while the turkey keeps it relatively lean. Either way, this is a wonderful alternative to all of you who love a pizza with sausage.

makes 2 pizzas, each 8 to 10 inches in diameter

Dough from Basic Pizza Dough recipe (page 168), or 2 premade 8- to 10-inch crusts

2 to 3 tablespoons extra virgin olive oil

½ pound ground turkey

½ pound ground pork

½ medium clove garlic, minced

1 cup Marinara Sauce (page 224)

¼ cup heavy cream

Salt and freshly ground black pepper to taste

Approximately 1 cup mozzarella, shredded

3 or 4 basil leaves, slivered

Preheat the oven to 400°F. Shape the dough as desired and place it on a greased baking sheet.

Put the olive oil in a large sauté pan over high heat for 30 seconds. Add the turkey and pork, and cook for a few minutes until it is completely browned. Sauté the garlic for a few moments, until it starts to turn golden brown. Add the Marinara Sauce and the cream, stir, and cook for about 1 minute, or until the sauce begins to boil. Remove from the heat and season with the salt and pepper.

Divide the contents of the sauté pan between the two pizza crusts, bake for 10 minutes, remove the pizzas from the oven, and dot each with as little or as much mozzarella as you like. Return the pizzas to the oven for about 10 minutes, or until the bottoms of the crusts have browned and the cheese has melted. Remove the pizzas from the oven, sprinkle with the basil, cut into slices, and serve.

PIZZA WITH SAUSAGE, PEPPERS, AND ONIONS

I COULDN'T RESIST putting in my own version of yet another Italian pizza classic. After all, this combination has been served alone, in a sandwich, or over pasta countless times. I knew that it would be delicious over pizza as well.

makes 2 pizzas, each 8 to 10 inches in diameter

Dough from Basic Pizza Dough recipe (page 168), or 2 premade 8- to 10-inch crusts

3 to 4 tablespoons extra virgin olive oil

1 pound sweet Italian sausage, parboiled and cut into 1-inch pieces

1 medium clove garlic, minced

2 Italian peppers, cut into 1/4-inch strips

1 large white onion, cut into 1/4-inch strips

2 plum tomatoes, diced

Salt and freshly ground black pepper to taste

Approximately 1 cup mozzarella, shredded

1 tablespoon Italian (flat-leaf) parsley, stems removed and chopped

Preheat the oven to 400°F. Shape the dough as desired and place it on a greased baking sheet.

Put the oil in a large sauté pan over high heat for about 30 seconds. Cook the parboiled sausage in the hot oil for a few minutes, until the meat is completely browned. Sauté the garlic for a few seconds, until it begins to turn golden brown, then cook the peppers and onion for 1 to 2 minutes more, until they begin to brown and soften. Add the tomatoes, and cook for about 30 seconds, until they begin to soften and release their juices. Remove from the heat and season with the salt and pepper.

Divide the contents of the sauté pan between the two pizza crusts, bake for 10 minutes, remove the pizzas from the oven, and dot each with as little or as much mozzarella as you like. Return the pizzas to the oven for about 10 minutes, or until the bottoms of the crusts have browned and the cheese has melted. Remove the pizzas from the oven, sprinkle with parsley, cut into slices, and serve.

8

TWO menus

COMFORT FOOD AND AN
INTIMATE DINNER FOR TWO

⊠

AS I WRITE this chapter, the residents of Ridgefield, Conn., the small New England town where I live and where my restaurant, Biscotti, is located, are preparing for the first major snowstorm of the season. I'm sure the grocery stores are packed with people buying all the goodies they will want on hand to help them feel cozy and comfortable while the storm rages.

Meanwhile, more and more people are stopping by the restaurant to buy my Super Mom Meals. Super Mom Meals are simple, basic Italian and American meals, such as Chicken Parmesan and meatloaf, made fresh, then frozen in packages to serve two or more. Why do meals like these make us feel so good? Because they taste good in a simple, honest kind of way. Comfort food does more than just taste good, it evokes memories of when life was unrushed and uncomplicated. It reminds us to just stop and enjoy the present, the food we're eating, and the people we love who are sharing it with us.

Though for some, tomato soup and grilled cheese sandwiches make the perfect comfort meal, for something a little more adventurous, I encourage you to try part or all of the menu below. Make this meal for your family or close friends or make it for a special evening when the storm is blowing outside, the fire is blazing inside, the table is set for two, and the aroma from the kitchen is intoxicating.

Sometimes, the desire for opulence is stronger than the desire for comfort. There may be romance in the air, or celebration, or both. The second menu is meant for that kind of extravagance. It's not a meal for everyday eating, so make it when the time is right. For an intimate, exotic dinner such as this one, go all out. Use your best china. Light the candles. Turn on your favorite soft music. Open that expensive bottle of wine. After all, you are waiting to propose or waiting to be proposed to. Or maybe you just want that special someone to know of your love.

⊠

COMFORT FOOD

Sautéed Mussels with Garlic Crostini

Sautéed Spinach Salad with Crispy Pancetta and Balsamic Vinegar

Hand-Rolled Lasagna with Sausage and Peppers

Sautéed Apple "Pie" with Biscotti Crumb Topping

⊠

SAUTÉED MUSSELS WITH GARLIC CROSTINI

THIS RECIPE IS simple, fast, and satisfying, all the criteria for comfort food. Furthermore, mussels are inexpensive and plentiful year round. If you don't like mussels, substitute clams or another type of shellfish. The crostini are simply slices of baguette bread rubbed with garlic and oil.

makes 2 servings

4 to 5 tablespoons extra virgin olive oil

Pinch of red pepper flakes

24 mussels, cleaned and debearded

1 medium clove garlic, minced

¼ cup White Wine Sauce (page 222)

½ cup fish broth

2 basil leaves, sliced

1 tablespoon Italian (flat-leaf) parsley, stems removed and chopped

Salt and freshly ground black pepper to taste

4 to 6 slices baguette, each slice about ¼ inch thick,
   toasted and rubbed with 1 cut garlic clove

Put the oil and red pepper flakes in a large sauté pan over high heat for about 30 seconds, or until the oil is hot but not smoking. Cook the mussels for about 2 to 3 minutes, until they begin to open. Sauté the garlic briefly, until it begins to turn golden brown, then add the White Wine Sauce and cook for 1 minute more. Add the fish broth, cover, and cook for 2 to 3 minutes, until the mussels have fully opened and turned opaque. Add the herbs, remove the pan from the heat, and season with the salt and pepper. Put the mussels and sauce in a warm serving bowl, top with the baguette slices. Serve at once.

SAUTÉED SPINACH SALAD with CRISPY PANCETTA and BALSAMIC VINEGAR

THIS IS A wonderful alternative to a fresh, cold spinach salad. It uses the same basic ingredients but substitutes pancetta, or Italian bacon, which is thicker and moister than American bacon. Like everything else in these pages, it is sautéed and served warm. If you cannot get pancetta, use slab bacon instead.

makes 2 servings

2 tablespoons extra virgin olive oil

Pinch of red pepper flakes

1 package (10 ounces) fresh spinach

½ medium clove garlic, minced

2 tablespoons chicken broth

2 slices (⅛ inch thick) pancetta, cut in medium dice

3 tablespoons good-quality balsamic vinegar

Salt and freshly ground black pepper to taste

Put the olive oil and red pepper flakes in a large sauté pan over high heat for about 30 seconds, or until the oil is hot but not smoking. Add the spinach and cook for about 1 minute or until the leaves are just beginning to wilt. (Don't worry if the pile in the pan is high; the leaves will wilt quickly and the pile will become much smaller.) Add the garlic and cook just until it begins to turn golden brown. Add the chicken broth, cook for 1 minute more, transfer the spinach to serving plates, and return the skillet to the heat.

Cook the diced pancetta for 2 to 3 minutes, or until it becomes crispy. Turn off the heat, and transfer the pancetta with a slotted spoon to a paper towel.

To serve, top the spinach with the pancetta, drizzle with balsamic vinegar, and add a bit more oil, if desired. Season with salt and pepper.

HAND-ROLLED LASAGNA
WITH SAUSAGE AND PEPPERS

W E HAVE BEEN making a different hand-rolled lasagna each day since the restaurant opened. It is one of our signature dishes. This is true comfort food made fancy, with each noodle filled individually and hand-rolled. Because each piece can be customized, if someone doesn't like peppers, for example, we can make just that roll without peppers. If someone doesn't eat meat, that person's piece can be made without meat. But I highly recommend filling each piece with the ricotta-béchamel mixture in this recipe. This base gives each piece a creamy taste that just melts in your mouth but isn't as heavy as ricotta alone. Making hundreds of hand-rolled pieces each week has taught me that the filling is one reason for the popularity of this dish. The best part is that you can make lasagna for just two people without having to make a full pan of the more common flat, layered lasagna. This dish is also filled with sausage and peppers, the ultimate Italian comfort food.

makes 2 servings

4 lasagna noodles

I cup Marinara Sauce (page 224)

I cup Ricotta/Béchamel Sauce (page 84)

3 to 4 tablespoons olive oil

½ pound sweet Italian sausage, casing removed

I medium clove garlic, minced

I red bell pepper, thinly sliced

Chicken broth or water

Salt and freshly ground black pepper to taste

SIMPLY **sauté**

½ cup mozzarella cheese, shredded

1 tablespoon Italian (flat-leaf) parsley, stems removed and chopped

2 basil leaves, sliced (optional garnish)

Cook the lasagna noodles in a large pot of boiling, salted water for about 10 minutes, and drain while the noodles are still firm. Rinse the noodles under cold water to stop further cooking (remember, they will cook more in the oven.) Preheat the oven to 350°F.

Put half the oil in a large sauté pan over high heat for about 30 seconds. Brown the sausage meat in the hot oil for 4 to 5 minutes, taking care not to overstir the meat and cause improper browning. Remove the pan from the heat, and, using a slotted spoon, transfer the sausage to paper towels, keeping the oil in the pan.

Return the pan to high heat and sauté the garlic for about 30 seconds, until it begins to turn golden brown. Sauté the pepper strips for 2 to 3 minutes. If the peppers are browning too quickly, add a splash of chicken broth or water to slow down cooking, then continue to cook until peppers are soft but still firm. Remove from heat, and season with the salt and pepper.

To assemble, lay each noodle flat on a cutting board or clean surface. Spread each ingredient over each of the flat noodles as follows: one-quarter of the ricotta-béchamel mixture, one-quarter of the meat, about 3 tablespoons of Marinara Sauce, and one-quarter of the mozzarella.

Roll each noodle from one end to the other to form a roll. Coat the bottom of a small baking pan with a bit of Marinara Sauce. Place the rolled lasagna into the pan. Bake in the preheated oven for about 20 minutes, or until the filling is hot and the cheese begins to melt.

To serve, place 2 pieces of lasagna in the center of each serving plate, top with additional Marinara Sauce, and sprinkle with the parsley. If desired, garnish with fresh basil.

SAUTÉED APPLE 'PIE' WITH
BISCOTTI CRUMB TOPPING

WE CAN'T GET more comfortable than eating apple pie. Yes, you can sauté this interpretation of apple pie. The result is a wonderful twist on an old favorite.

makes 2 servings

FOR THE APPLE "PIE":

  2 tablespoons butter

  I Granny Smith apple, peeled and cut in medium slices

  I tablespoon dry white wine

  2 tablespoons light brown sugar

FOR THE TOPPING:

  2 tablespoons butter

  I biscotti cookie (use your favorite), crumbled

  2 tablespoons white wine

  I tablespoon White Wine Sauce (page 222)

FOR SERVING:

  Ground cinnamon to taste

  Caramel sauce and or whipped cream (optional)

  Fresh mint, for garnish

Preheat the oven to 200°F.

Melt the 2 tablespoons of butter for the "pie" in a medium sauté pan over medium-low heat, and cook the apple slices for about 1 minute. Add the wine and brown sugar, and cook for 1 more minute, or until the apple slices have softened but are still

SIMPLY **sauté**

firm. Remove from heat, transfer the apples slices to a baking dish and keep warm in the oven.

To make the topping, melt the 2 tablespoons of butter in the same sauté pan, also over medium-low heat. Cook the cookie crumbs for about 1 minute, or until the crumbs begin to brown, add the wine and cook for another minute, then add the White Wine Sauce and cook briefly, until the cookies have absorbed the sauce. Remove from heat.

To serve, divide the apple slices between two serving plates, top each with the cookie mixture and sprinkle with cinnamon. If desired, drizzle with caramel sauce and top each with whipped cream and a sprig of mint.

⊠

AN INTIMATE DINNER FOR TWO

Sautéed Wild Mushrooms with Sun-Dried Tomatoes and Brandy

over Heart-Shaped Polenta

Sautéed String Bean Salad with Beets and Gorgonzola

Salmon à la Vodka with Caviar over Fettuccine

Fresh Pears in Red Wine

⊠

SAUTÉED WILD MUSHROOMS WITH SUN-DRIED TOMATOES AND BRANDY OVER HEART-SHAPED POLENTA

OKAY, SO IT sounds a little corny making heart-shaped polenta. But if we can't be corny when we're in love, when can we be? Rest assured, though, the taste is anything but corny (except for the polenta, which, after all, is cornmeal). Still, it's exotic and full of flavor.

makes 2 servings

3 to 4 tablespoons extra virgin olive oil

Pinch of red pepper flakes

1 large portabello mushroom, stems removed and sliced

6 cremino mushrooms, sliced or quartered

6 shiitake mushrooms, stems removed and sliced

½ medium clove garlic, minced

3 to 4 tablespoons brandy

3 to 4 tablespoons White Wine Sauce (page 222)

¼ cup dry-packed sun-dried tomatoes, slivered

¼ cup Marinara Sauce (page 224)

¼ cup chicken broth

1 tablespoon heavy cream

Salt and freshly ground black pepper to taste

1 box (1.1 pounds) instant polenta

Basil, for garnish

1 tablespoon Italian (flat-leaf) parsley, stems removed and chopped

Put the olive oil and red pepper flakes in a large sauté pan over high heat for about 30 seconds, or until the oil is hot but not smoking. Cook the mushrooms until they are softened, about 2 to 3 minutes, then sauté the garlic, just until it begins to turn golden brown. Add the brandy, White Wine Sauce, sun-dried tomatoes, Marinara Sauce, and chicken broth. Stir and cook for 1 more minute, until the sauce begins to boil. Reduce the heat, add the cream, and cook for another minute to thicken the sauce. Remove the pan from the heat, and season with the salt and pepper.

Meanwhile, cook the polenta according to the package directions. Put the mixture on a 10 x 15-inch baking sheet, and refrigerate until firm, about 15 to 20 minutes. If you have a heart-shaped cookie cutter, use it to cut the polenta. If you don't, make a paper cutout of a heart, lay it over the polenta and cut the shape with a knife.

To serve, place each polenta heart on an individual plate and top each with half the mushroom mixture. Garnish with basil or other decorative leaf and sprinkle with the parsley.

SAUTÉED STRING BEAN SALAD
WITH BEETS AND GORGONZOLA

WHEN I FIRST thought to try this combination, I wasn't thrilled with using beets because I don't particularly care for them. Still, I was intrigued with the colors of this dish, so I decided to try it. To my surprise, it was more than just a pretty dish. It was delicious. It can also be made ahead of time. Serve this dish as the salad course or as a side dish.

¼ cup extra virgin olive oil

Pinch of red pepper flakes

½ pound string beans, cleaned, trimmed and microwaved for about 5 minutes

½ medium clove garlic, minced

¼ cup chicken broth

1 medium beet, thinly sliced and microwaved for about 2 minutes in a microwave-safe container until softened yet still firm

2 tablespoons Gorgonzola cheese

¼ cup good-quality balsamic vinegar

Put half the olive oil and the red pepper flakes in a large sauté pan over high heat for about 30 seconds. Sauté the parcooked beans for about 2 minutes, until they are slightly browned, then sauté them briefly with the garlic, just until the garlic begins to turn golden brown. Add the chicken broth and cook for 1 more minute. Remove the pan from the heat, transfer the beans to a bowl, and refrigerate them until chilled.

Place the string beans on a platter and top with the beets, using a slotted spoon to remove them from their juices in the container. Dot with the Gorgonzola and drizzle with the remaining olive oil and the balsamic vinegar.

SALMON À LA VODKA
WITH CAVIAR OVER FETTUCCINE

I ENJOYED A dish similar to this when I was in Florence. The restaurant was lively and rustic and just a short, romantic walk from the Arno River. This time, however, my romantic notions remained in my head, for my company that night, lovely as it was, included my two children. But when the time is right, this is a wonderful dish for a romantic evening. I duplicated the dish I had in Florence, using my recipe for vodka sauce and using large chunks of fresh salmon instead of small flakes, which got lost in the rich vodka sauce. Finish it with a dollop of good caviar and you'll have a truly exotic dish that's surprisingly easy to prepare.

makes 2 servings

½ pound fettuccine

3 to 4 tablespoons extra virgin olive oil

Pinch of red pepper flakes

½ pound salmon filet, skinned and sliced into 6 to 8 pieces

½ medium clove garlic, minced

¼ cup vodka

I cup Marinara Sauce (page 224)

¼ cup fish broth

¼ cup heavy cream

Salt and freshly ground black pepper to taste

2 tablespoons black caviar

2 basil leaves, cut in ¼-inch slices

Cook the pasta according to package directions in a large pot of boiling, salted water.

While the pasta cooks, put the olive oil and red pepper flakes in a large sauté pan over high heat for about 30 seconds, or until the oil is hot but not smoking. Cook the salmon pieces for about 1 minute on each side. When each piece begins to brown, turn it and brown the second side for 1 minute, then add the garlic and cook for a few seconds, just until the garlic begins to turn golden brown.

Turn off the heat and carefully add the vodka, being aware that the alcohol will make a small flame. Return the pan to the heat and cook for about 1 minute, giving the vodka time to burn off. Add the Marinara Sauce and fish broth, stir, and cook for about 2 more minutes, until the sauce begins to boil. Reduce the heat, add the cream, and simmer until the salmon is done to your liking and the sauce has thickened. Season with salt and pepper.

To serve, drain the pasta and toss it in a large bowl with half the liquid portion of the sauce. Divide the pasta between individual serving plates and top with the rest of the liquid sauce and the chunks of salmon. Top with a dollop of caviar, sprinkle with the basil slices, and serve immediately.

caviar

CAVIAR IS ONE of those foods that sounds exotic and expensive, and it can be both. It's also easy enough to buy moderately priced—or even inexpensive—varieties of caviar. The point is, don't be put off by a recipe just because its use of caviar makes it sound beyond your reach. A little bit goes a long way.

FRESH PEARS IN RED WINE

THIS IS WONDERFUL as is or served with vanilla ice cream.

- 2 tablespoons butter
- 1 ripe pear, any variety, peeled and cut into medium slices
- 2 tablespoons dry red wine
- 2 tablespoons light brown sugar
- 2 tablespoons White Wine Sauce (page 222)
- Vanilla ice cream (optional)
- 2 sprigs fresh mint and whipped cream (optional garnishes)

Melt the butter in a small or medium sauté pan over medium-low heat and sauté the pear slices in the melted butter for about 1 minute, or until the pears begin to turn golden brown. Add the wine and brown sugar and cook for another minute, until the pear slices begin to caramelize and soften. Add the White Wine Sauce and cook briefly until the pears are cooked but still firm. Divide the mixture between 2 serving plates. Add ice cream, if desired, and garnish with mint and/or whipped cream.

9

SAUTÉ desserts

⊠

I HAVE THE most wonderful pastry chef at my restaurant. Her name is Diane Ferguson. Every day, Diane makes cheesecakes, cobblers, tarts, crème brûlée, and, of course, biscotti. I don't even think about desserts. So when I wanted to include a dessert chapter for this book, I was a bit skeptical, for I thought that sautéing desserts might be too much of a stretch, even for the versatile technique of sauté. I was wrong.

My foray into sautéing desserts opened up a whole new area of possibilities for my sauté pan. It offered the opportunity to work with a whole new set of ingredients and it redefined and expanded my vision of heavenly desserts.

As I started to sauté various combinations, I was amazed at the results. They're easy, fun, and totally unexpected. Here are the fruits (and there are lots of those in this chapter) of my labors.

SAUTÉED PEACHES IN PEACH SCHNAPPS

HIS IS A wonderfully delicious twist on the elegantly simple peaches-and-cream dessert.

makes 2 servings

2 tablespoons butter

2 fresh or frozen peaches, sliced

¼ cup peach schnapps

2 tablespoons heavy cream

Whipped cream

2 sprigs mint (optional garnish)

Ice cream (optional)

Melt the butter in a small or medium sauté pan over medium-low heat. Sauté the peach slices in the melted butter for about 1 minute, or until they begin to turn golden brown. Turn off the heat and carefully add the schnapps, being aware that a flame will probably result. Turn the heat on again, cook the sauce for about 1 minute, and add the cream. Remove from the heat. Serve warm with whipped cream and a sprig of mint, or refrigerate for about 5 minutes until the sauce is the thickness of caramel, and serve over ice cream.

SAUTÉED ICE CREAM WRAPPED
IN A DELICATE CRÊPE

WHEN I TOLD my staff I was going to sauté ice cream, not only did they think I was nuts, they thought I couldn't do it. "Ha!" I said. "Just watch." This is an example of the intuitive powers of a chef. A chef just knows when something will work, even if he or she has never tried it. Well, usually, anyway. This recipe works beautifully. It may, however, take a few tries to get the crêpes to come out just right: golden brown on the outside, the ice cream just beginning to melt on the inside. Play with the pan temperature until you get it just right and find the perfect time to take the crêpes out of the pan. Make a few extra for practice and enjoy eating and sharing your "mistakes."

makes 4 crêpes, 2 to 4 servings

4 scoops vanilla ice cream (or your favorite flavor)

4 pastry crêpes, each about 8 inches in diameter (store bought, or follow the simple recipe on opposite page)

2 tablespoons butter

1 tablespoon extra virgin olive oil

¼ cup raspberry or strawberry jam, melted (add a bit of water if too thick)

Whipped cream

2 sprigs mint (optional garnish)

Put 1 scoop of ice cream in the center of each crêpe, and roll the crêpes into a cylinder, tucking in the ends to completely enclose the ice cream. Freeze until the ice cream is extremely hard. At the same time, place 2 dessert plates in the freezer.

Melt the butter with the oil in a large sauté pan over high heat, heating until the mixture is very hot but not smoking. The oil will help keep the butter from burning, but if the butter turns brown, your heat was too high, so start again and use lower heat. Keep the crêpes in the freezer until you're ready to sauté. Then cook the crêpes, seam sides up, in the hot oil until they're golden brown, about 30 seconds. Flip the crêpes and brown them on the second sides. Remove the finished crêpes from the pan and place two on each cold dessert plate. Drizzle 1 tablespoon of jam over each crêpe, top with whipped cream, garnish with mint, if desired, and serve immediately.

NOTE: I suggest you buy these crêpes already prepared, usually from the frozen-foods section of your supermarket. Though crêpes are relatively easy to prepare, it doesn't make sense to make a batch of batter for 4 crêpes.

213

crêpes

½ cup all purpose flour

½ cup milk

Pinch of salt

1 large egg

1 tablespoon melted butter or vegetable oil, plus 1 teaspoon butter or vegetable oil
  spray

Combine the flour, milk, and salt and beat into a smooth paste. Blend in the egg and the 1 tablespoon of melted butter or vegetable oil. In a small nonstick pan, over medium heat, melt one-quarter teaspoon of butter or vegetable oil spray, followed by a tablespoon of batter. Swirl it around until it covers the bottom of the pan in a thin layer. The bottom will dry in less than a minute. Take a rubber spatula and loosen the edges of the crêpe and turn. Cook for 10 to 15 seconds more and remove from the pan. Repeat until you have the number of crêpes desired. Separate each crêpe with a small piece of wax paper.

BANANAS IN CREAM AND HAZELNUT LIQUEUR

THIS IS A variation on the peaches-and-schnapps recipe, but with bananas and a different liqueur. It's great served alone, with ice cream, or over a slice of your favorite pound cake.

makes 2 servings

2 tablespoons butter

2 bananas, cut in medium slices

¼ cup hazelnut liqueur (Frangelico)

2 tablespoons heavy cream

¼ cup hazelnuts, chopped

4 sprigs fresh mint and whipped cream (garnishes)

Ice cream or pound cake (optional)

Melt the butter in a small or medium sauté pan over medium-low heat. Cook the banana slices in the melted butter for about 30 seconds, then, with the heat turned off, add the liqueur, being aware that a flame may result. Return the pan to the heat and cook for 30 seconds. Add the cream, cook for 1 minute longer, and remove from the heat.

Sprinkle with the hazelnuts and garnish with whipped cream and mint before serving warm, or refrigerate for about 5 minutes, until the sauce is the consistency of caramel, and serve over ice cream or pound cake.

SAUTÉED POUND CAKE
WITH FRESH STRAWBERRIES

T HIS RECIPE IS incredibly simple. Just sauté your favorite pound cake to a golden brown and serve it warm, topped with fresh, ripe strawberries. If strawberries are out of season, use any ripe berry you can find. Top it off with fresh whipped cream and a sprig of mint, and you'll have produced a simple masterpiece.

makes 4 servings

  2 tablespoons butter

  4 slices pound cake

  8 strawberries, cleaned and sliced

  4 sprigs fresh mint and whipped cream (garnishes)

Melt the butter in a large sauté pan over medium heat. Brown the slices of pound cake in the melted butter for about 1 minute per side, or just until golden brown, remove from heat, and put the cake on a serving platter or individual plate. Garnish each slice with fresh berries and, if desired, whipped cream and mint.

CREAM CHEESE–STUFFED FRENCH TOAST

T HIS FRENCH TOAST is good enough to satisfy a sweet tooth, so it can easily be served as a dessert. I taught this recipe to sixth, seventh, and eighth graders in my cooking class series, "Beyond Peanut Butter and Jelly." They took to it like bees to honey.

makes 2 large or 4 small servings

3 medium eggs, beaten

¼ cup whole milk

I teaspoon vanilla extract

¼ cup cream cheese, whipped or softened

4 slices challah bread, each slice ½ inch thick

4 tablespoons (½ stick) butter

Maple syrup

8 fresh strawberries

Whipped cream (for garnish)

Fresh mint (optional garnish)

Beat the eggs in a medium mixing bowl, add the milk and vanilla, and beat to combine. Spread the cream cheese between 2 slices of bread and dip the "sandwiches" in the egg mixture.

Melt 2 tablespoons of the butter in a large sauté pan over medium heat, and brown the "sandwiches" for about 1 minute on each side. Repeat, using the remaining butter, with the second "sandwich." Put the "sandwiches" on a microwave-safe platter, and microwave for 30 seconds to ensure the filling is soft. Cut each "sandwich" in half diagonally, drizzle with syrup, top with berries and whipped cream, and, if desired, mint.

SAUTÉED MIXED DRY FRUIT
WITH AMARETTO

T HIS IS A perfect dish for winter when flavorful, ripe, fresh fruit is not readily available. Sautéed dried fruits make a delicious sauce. I have sautéed
dried fruits in white wine sauce along with center-cut pork loin and served the mixture over risotto many times at the restaurant for an interestingly delicious special
that continues to be requested year after year by satisfied diners. I've made a few
changes to turn that idea into a dessert. One is to serve it over ice cream. But if you
want to skip the calories in the ice cream, serve it alone or over a piece of sugar-free
pound cake.

makes 4 servings

2 tablespoons butter

1 cup mixed dried fruit (apricots, peaches, plums, prunes, apples)

¼ cup amaretto

¼ cup White Wine Sauce (page 222)

¼ cup almonds, slivered

Ice cream or pound cake

Mint leaves, whipped cream (garnishes)

Melt the butter in a large sauté pan over medium heat and cook the dried fruits in the
melted butter for about 1 minute, until they are golden brown. Turn off the heat, and
add the amaretto, being aware that the alcohol may produce a sudden flame. Return
the pan to the heat, stir, add the White Wine Sauce, and cook for about 1 more
minute, until the sauce comes to a boil. Remove the pan from the heat, and put
the pan contents on serving plates. Top with the almonds and serve over your favorite
ice cream or pound cake. If desired, garnish with mint and whipped cream.

RASPBERRIES AND ORANGES IN LIQUEUR

BY NOW, I suppose you're beginning to suspect that the combinations for sautéing fruits can be endless. You're right. Just choose your favorite fruit, find a complementary liqueur, and, voilà, you have an instant dessert! This particular combination is fabulous.

makes 4 servings

2 tablespoons butter

½ pint fresh raspberries

2 oranges, peeled and sliced

¼ cup raspberry-flavored liqueur

¼ cup White Wine Sauce (page 222)

¼ cup orange juice

Ice cream

Melt the butter in a large sauté pan over medium-low heat, and cook the raspberries and orange slices in the melted butter for about 30 seconds. Add the liqueur, White Wine Sauce, and orange juice to the pan, and cook for 30 seconds more, or until the ingredients are combined and begin to thicken and the sauce comes to a boil. Serve warm immediately, or refrigerate until the sauce is the consistency of caramel and serve over ice cream.

10

FIVE STAPLE recipes

FOR CREATING SAUTÉ MAGIC

❈

EVERY GREAT CHEF starts with stocks, sauces, and broths to create more intricate sauces. A wonderful basic sauce or stock will significantly enhance the flavor of almost any dish. I have two that I use constantly—White Wine Sauce (my own creation) and Marinara Sauce. In this chapter, you'll learn how to make those two simple but important sauces as well as chicken, vegetable, and fish broths that you will use in almost everything you cook from this book (and many other books, too).

Besides being easy to make, these sauces can be easy to use. Freeze them in various sizes—from ice-cube trays to quart containers—to be used as needed in the recipes. The broths can be purchased, but they are easy to make yourself and always more flavorful if you do.

white wine sauce

THE EXACT THICKNESS of the White Wine Sauce is not critical, since that can be adjusted in the sauté pan. Thinning the sauce is a little easier than making it thicker, so you might prefer to err on the side of thickness. To thin the sauce, simply add a bit more broth. To thicken it, either cook the sauce longer in the stockpot or sauté pan so some liquid evaporates and the sauce reduces or add more flour. Adding flour to thicken any sauce is best started in a separate bowl. Mix a few tablespoons of flour with about ¼ cup of chicken broth and stir until it reaches the consistency of a smooth, thick paste, free of any lumps. Then add another ¼ cup of broth and stir until it reaches the consistency of a thin paste. Add this paste a spoonful at a time until the sauce reaches the consistency you desire. This sauce can also be made with vegetable broth.

WHITE WINE SAUCE

THIS IS WHERE you'll find a lot of the sauté magic. I call this sauce my "blank canvas" because it picks up the flavors of whatever ingredients are in your pan—meat, fish, or vegetables. Best of all, the sauce is just the background. It never dominates the flavor, instead, enhancing it and adding a creamy texture to whatever you are cooking. I discovered it by accident, and what a happy accident it turned out to be. I was trying to make a white wine sauce directly in the sauté pan by adding wine, flour, and chicken broth. It quickly became my favorite, so I began making it in large quantities and simply added a little to the ingredients in my sauté pan. You'll use this sauce with many of the recipes in this book. It's easy to make and you can freeze it in small containers so it's readily available whenever you need it. I'm confident that it will become a favorite of yours, too.

makes 5 to 6 cups

½ cup extra virgin olive oil

½ cup unbleached white flour

1 cup dry white wine

4 cups chicken broth

Salt and freshly ground black pepper to taste (see note)

Pour the olive oil into a 4- to 5-quart saucepan over medium heat, then add the flour and stir with a wire whisk until all the flour is dissolved and the mixture looks like a paste. Reduce the heat and slowly add the wine; the mixture will start to thicken quickly. Continue to stir and remove from the heat, if necessary, until all the wine has been mixed in. Slowly pour in the chicken broth while you continue to stir.

Simmer, uncovered, for approximately 45 minutes, or until the taste of alcohol is no longer present in the sauce.

Freeze in containers of various sizes, including some in an ice-cube tray to allow easy small additions to sauces. It can stay in the freezer for 6 months or more.

NOTE: Be sparing with the salt and pepper. It's better to underseason this sauce, because you will season it again in the sauté pan.

NOTE: If this (or any) sauce ever has lumps caused by undissolved flour, just pass the sauce through a sieve or a mesh strainer. It will come out lump-free.

QUICK SAUCE VARIATION: You can make a quick White Wine Sauce right in the sauté pan while you cook the other ingredients. Simply add ¼ cup of white wine and 2 tablespoons of flour to the pan juices and stir until you have a smooth paste. Slowly add ½ to 1 cup of chicken broth, depending on how thick you want the sauce to be, and cook for about 3 to 4 minutes.

MARINARA SAUCE

M ASTER THIS SAUCE and you're well on your way to being a terrific Italian cook. In my opinion, you can always tell whether you have found a great Italian restaurant by the quality of its marinara. It's one of the simplest sauces to make, yet one of the most difficult to make great. Only a few ingredients go into it, so each one plays a big part in the final result and must therefore be of the highest quality. I like to think that marinara sauce has in it something of the sea. My grandmother passed onto my mother, and she to me, a recipe using anchovies to flavor the sauce, and I have always made my sauce this way. I urge you to do the same, even if you don't like anchovies. You'd never know they were there, yet they add wonderful flavor.

makes 7 cups

3 to 4 tablespoons extra virgin olive oil

I small yellow onion, diced

2 anchovy fillets, chopped

I medium clove garlic, minced

3 cans (28 ounces each) whole peeled plum tomatoes (or crushed or diced tomatoes) in their own juice, coarsely chopped or broken up by hand (do not put through a food processor, which will affect taste and color), hard cores removed and discarded

2 or 3 whole basil leaves

I cup water

Salt and freshly ground black pepper to taste

Heat the olive oil in a 4- to 5-quart saucepan over medium heat for about 30 seconds. Cook the onion and anchovies in the hot oil for about 2 minutes, until they are soft.

SIMPLY **sauté**

Sauté the garlic for about 30 seconds, or until it begins to brown. Remove the pan from the heat and add the tomatoes and basil leaves. Bring to a boil, pour in the water (the sauce will lose a lot of liquid during cooking), and reduce the heat to low.

Partially cover the pan to allow steam to escape, and cook for approximately 1½ to 2 hours, until you have a thick, rich sauce. Stir occasionally to prevent bits of the tomatoes from sinking to the bottom of the pan and burning. Season with salt and pepper.

QUICK SAUCE VARIATION: For a quick tomato sauce that is still delicious, buy canned tomatoes (available under a variety of brand names) that are labeled "recipe ready" or "kitchen ready." This sauce will take about 25 to 35 minutes to prepare.

what's the difference?

IS THERE A difference between tomato sauce and marinara sauce? In America, the two are used interchangeably. I could not find any information on the origins of marinara sauce, and a search of marinara and tomato sauce resulted in similar recipes (though some tomato sauces also add carrots and celery). However, a long-time restaurateur from Naples told me that marinara sauce was originally made for the sailors (the *marinaro*) of that region, and was used as a sauce for pizza.

the very best

I OFTEN TELL my students this story, about the best marinara sauce I had ever eaten. I had been living in Italy, going to art school, and was in Rome for a few days before returning to the States. I had little money but wanted to dine in a nice restaurant. The one I chose had white tablecloths and a courtyard garden. I ordered only a first-course pasta—the least expensive one—and a bottle of mineral water. The waiter was gracious, even though he must have known he wouldn't be getting a large tip. I tried to act as though I could have ordered anything on the menu, but the penne marinara was the only dish I wanted. Little did I know, this dish would be one of the most memorable of my life, even many years and many expensive restaurant meals later.

The sauce was light and sweet with bits of tomato pieces. It was so fresh that it tasted as if the sauce was made from tomatoes just picked off the vine, and it perfectly coated the ridges in the penne. The pasta was smothered with fresh-slivered basil, and each bite exploded with flavor.

I have never had a marinara sauce as good in any restaurant since. Often it's the simplest sauces that are the most difficult to get right. There are so few ingredients and cooking steps that each must be perfect, so use the best tomatoes, the finest olive oil, and the freshest basil. As you stir the sauce, add a lot of love. Your family and friends will surely feel it.

stock vs. broth

YOU'D BE ASTONISHED at how much research went into the decision of whether to use the word "stock" or "broth" to describe the concoction that's used in so many recipes. I decided on "broth." The reason: It seems that you *make* stock while you *buy* broth and despite the recipes I offer for chicken, vegetable, and fish stock or broth, I know that most of you, most of the time, will go to your supermarket and buy some canned liquid. At the market, those cans contain "broth," so that's what I'll call it here. Even *I* buy them, confining my stock making to times when I'm making soup anyway. Homemade is always better, and you can always control what goes into your liquid. The canned products available today are quite good, so buy them. They'll be called "broth" both on the shelves and in this book.

CHICKEN BROTH

C HICKEN BROTH IS invaluable for adding flavor and additional liquid to almost any sauce or non-seafood dish. It's a staple in every professional chef's kitchen. Whether you use fresh, canned, frozen, or granulated, once you start cooking with chicken broth, you'll never be without it. It's widely available in any supermarket in its many varieties, but it's also easy to make from scratch. Besides being easy, it has the advantage of allowing you to control the amount of added salt (many commercial brands add more than you may want) as well as eliminating any preservatives and additives, such as MSG.

makes approximately 3 quarts

1 whole chicken or 3 pounds chicken wings, backs, and necks
4 quarts cold water
2 yellow onions, peeled and halved
2 carrots, peeled and coarsely chopped
2 celery stalks, coarsely chopped
6 to 8 sprigs Italian (flat-leaf) parsley, stems included
1 teaspoon salt
1 teaspoon coarsely ground black pepper
2 to 3 fresh basil leaves

Place all the ingredients in a large stockpot (6 to 8 quarts) over high heat, bring to a boil, and skim any froth from the surface. Reduce the heat and simmer, uncovered, for approximately 2 hours, skimming froth as needed. Strain the broth though a sieve or mesh strainer, discarding any chicken bones and vegetables. (If you used a whole chicken, remove any meat from the bones and use the meat in a soup or salad.)

Allow the broth to cool, and store in small covered containers in the refrigerator for up to 5 days or in the freezer for up to 4 months.

SIMPLYsaut茅

FISH BROTH

Fish broth adds flavor and additional liquid to seafood dishes and sauces, just as chicken broth does for poultry, meats, and vegetables. While clam broth can be found in most supermarkets, canned fish broth can usually be found only in specialty gourmet shops. But it's easy to make yourself. Visit your local fish market or supermarket and ask for whitefish bones. There'll surely be plenty, and you will likely get them for free or for just a nominal charge. Like chicken and vegetable broths, it's a good idea to make a large batch and freeze it in various size containers—ice-cube trays for small amounts, 8- and 16-ounce containers for larger amounts.

makes approximately 6 cups

2 pounds whitefish bones, washed in cold water

2 quarts cold water

1 medium onion, peeled and quartered

1 cup dry white wine

½ bunch Italian (flat-leaf) parsley, with stems

1 teaspoon salt

1 teaspoon coarsely ground black pepper

4 fresh basil leaves

Place all ingredients in a large stockpot (6 to 8 quarts) over high heat, bring to a boil, and skim any froth from the surface. Reduce the heat and simmer, uncovered, for 1 hour. Strain through a sieve or mesh strainer into a large container, discarding bones and vegetables. Cool and store in small covered containers in the refrigerator for up to 5 days or in the freezer for up to 4 months.

VEGETABLE BROTH

VEGETABLE BROTH CAN be substituted for chicken or fish broth in any recipe in this book. This is good news for vegetarians. Commercially produced vegetable broth is available in many supermarkets, but, like chicken and fish broth, these broths tend to be saltier and contain other additives that homemade broth does not. It's easy to prepare this broth, so why not make a big batch and freeze it in different size containers so it's ready for various uses? Though the recipe below calls for specific vegetables, feel free to use whatever vegetables you have on hand.

makes approximately 6 cups

2 quarts cold water

1 yellow onion, quartered

2 large carrots, washed and quartered

2 large celery stalks, washed and chopped in 3-inch lengths

2 large ripe tomatoes, washed and quartered

2 large zucchini, washed and quartered

2 bell peppers, washed, seeds removed, and quartered

1 large bulb fennel, washed and chopped in 3-inch lengths

2 whole cloves garlic

4 sprigs Italian (flat-leaf) parsley, stems included

2 basil leaves

1 teaspoon salt

1 teaspoon coarsely ground black pepper

Place all the ingredients in a large stockpot (6 to 8 quarts) over high heat, bring to a boil, and skim any froth from the surface. Reduce the heat and simmer, uncovered, for 1 hour.

Strain through a sieve or mesh strainer into a large container, discarding the vegetables. Cool and store in small covered containers in the refrigerator for up to 5 days or in the freezer for up to 4 months.

choosing a broth

FISH BROTH IS the liquid you should add to a seafood dish. You should not add it to chicken or meat dishes or you risk putting a fishy taste where it doesn't belong. Chicken broth gives you a bit more latitude in that it's a perfect addition to chicken dishes and is just fine to add to meat dishes. Vegetable broth is the universal donor, welcome in any seafood, chicken, meat, or vegetable dish.

Acknowledgments

THERE ARE SO many people and experiences that have directly or indirectly helped me to create this book. I almost don't know where to start. First, I would like to thank Corwyn Anthony, my partner in the creation of our restaurant Biscotti, which molded the chef that lived within me and provided a rich and delicious forum for what resulted. You knew what I could do before I did. Thank you for believing in me.

To my children Teresa and Mathew who put up with the horrendous restaurant hours and all the fancy food they were forced to eat when all they really wanted was macaroni and cheese.

To my agent, Theresa Stefanidis, and my publisher Matthew Lore—no I'm not making this up—their names are the same as those of my children—still this "coincidence" did help to confirm my instincts that they were the right people for this project. I thank you for believing in this book and working with me to make it happen. Thanks also to Theresa's partner, Heather Bauccio; I know you spent countless hours working on the manuscript with Theresa.

I am especially grateful to my sister-in-law and a brilliant publicist, Jane Rohman, who nagged me into writing this book first, when I was hell-bent on writing another.

To Ken Bookman, whose skills as an editor provided the objectivity and attention to detail that did so much to pull this book together—thank you. And to Lisa Ekus, who I look so forward to working with to bring this book into the hands of its readers.

To my friend and astrologer Jill, who always seemed to provide the right guidance, just when I most needed it; and to my dear friend Dee, who never stopped believing in me, in anything. Thank you.

To the staff of Biscotti, who worked hard, year after year to make it the special place it is; with special thanks to my kitchen staff who do such a wonderful job making my food every day, with me or without me. Finally to all my customers. It is your continued enthusiasm for my food that makes me feel that I truly am expressing a gift. Thank you for the opportunity to share it.

One last acknowledgment: Special, special thanks to my four-burner stove for challenging me to go beyond what I thought was possible. You are forever etched in my memory.

—CHEF SILVIA

Index

237

238

239